STRUCTURING COOPERATIVE LEARNING:
Lesson Plans for Teachers
1987

Editors:

**Roger T. Johnson, David W. Johnson
and Edythe Johnson Holubec**

Design and
Production Editor:

Judy K. Bartlett

Interaction Book Company
7208 Cornelia Drive
Edina, MN 55435
(612) 831-9500

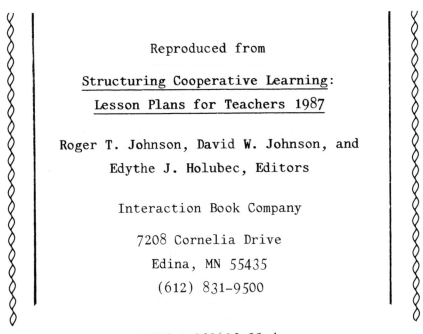

Dedication

Thanks are in order to Judy Bartlett, our office manager, who worked beyond the call of duty to put this handbook together and added all the touches that make such a difference.

We also wish to acknowledge the teachers who have structured cooperative learning groups in their classrooms, and have pushed their way through the barriers that stood in the way to transforming classrooms into places where students care about each other's learning. They deserve to be recognized for what they have done for the students they teach.

Cooperative Learning Center

The primary missions of the Cooperative Learning Center are to conduct research on cooperative learning and assist school districts, colleges, and other educational organizations in implementing cooperative learning. Priority is given to long-term programmatic efforts that organize existing knowledge of cooperation, generate and validate cooperation theory, develop cooperative learning strategies, and implement cooperative learning procedures into classrooms, schools, and other educational settings.

≈ Table of Contents ≈

Introduction

Teachers throughout North America are revitalizing the use of cooperative learning strategies in the classroom. Once a dominant factor in North American schools, cooperative learning procedures have been used infrequently for the past 25 years. That trend is now being reversed. For the past 10 years we have been part of a network of classroom teachers, public school administrators, college professors, and adult educators who are committed to implementing cooperative learning strategies in their schools and classrooms. Network members come from all parts of the United States and Canada and from Scandinavia, Australia, and several other countries. All subject areas and levels of education are represented. A considerable number of the members of the network have been part of our training at Sagamore Institute in the Adirondack Mountains. Other members teach in the school districts where we have trained teachers and administrators over a number of years. Some network members have been part of our graduate program at the University of Minnesota. Network members are educators who have (a) recognized the power in having students learn cooperatively, and (b) persevered in following that belief to success. All network members are affiliated with the Cooperative Learning Center and are people we think about a lot. We are fans of theirs and wish them continued success in structuring classrooms so that students care about each other and are committed to maximizing each other's learning.

Network members often express a desire to exchange lesson plans in order to provide each other with collaborative assistance. Curiosity as to what other members of the network were doing in their classrooms sparked interest in the creation of lesson plan handbooks. And many network members expressed a need to have sample lesson plans to give to workshop participants and colleagues who are just beginning to use cooperative learning strategies. To meet these needs a series of handbooks has been published.

This is the fifth in the series. It is a compilation of original lessons from network members all across the United States. The lessons are organized from the elementary school level to that of high school. The grade level and subject area of each lesson plan are designated. We have found that with just a bit of translation, the lessons can be taught at a range of age levels and taken from one subject and used in another. You should feel free to experiment, but keep in mind the basics of making a cooperative lesson work:

1. Specifying the academic and the collaborative skills objectives for the lesson.

2. Making decisions about placing students in learning groups (size of groups, who is in each group, materials for each group, arrangement of groups within the classroom, and roles assigned to group members).

3. Explaining the task, goal structure, and learning activity to the students (this includes clear positive interdependence,

individual accountability, criteria for success, and desired collaborative behaviors).

4. Monitoring the effectiveness of the cooperative learning groups and intervening to provide task assistance or to increase students' interpersonal and group skills.

5. Evaluating students' achievement and helping students analyze how well they collaborated with each other.

A good way to use this handbook is to browse through the lessons to obtain a sense of what types of lessons are included. Then, using the Table of Contents or the Index, select a lesson to read through carefully with the intention of teaching it (or using it as a springboard for a lesson of your own). You will find it interesting to examine a number of lessons to see how the teachers structured the positive interdependence among students and what monitoring procedures were used. The three articles at the beginning of the book review the procedures for structuring lessons cooperatively and summarize the rationale for doing so. More complete discussions may be found in **Circles of Learning--Revised Edition** (Johnson, Johnson and Holubec, 1987) and **Learning Together and Alone** (2nd ed.)(Johnson & Johnson, 1987). There are also two movies on implementing cooperative learning available.

If you wish to contribute to the next handbook, please let us know. Send us your favorite cooperative lessons. A sample format can be found in the final section of this handbook. The list of authors of the lesson plans is included so that you may contact them and ask them questions about implementing the lessons. We hope you do. We have enjoyed seeing the research promise come alive in their classrooms and appreciate their sharing their lessons with other teachers. **Thanks to all of you.**

R.T.J./D.W.J./E.J.H.

Cooperative Learning Center
University of Minnesota
202 Pattee
150 Pillsbury Drive, S.E.
Minneapolis, Minnesota 55455

(612) 624-7031

Introduction to
Cooperative Learning

Cooperative Learning

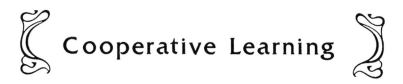

Roger T. Johnson and David W. Johnson

University of Minnesota

It is essentially the experience, the means, that fits human beings not to their external environment so much as to one another. Without the cooperation of its members society cannot survive, and the society of man has survived because the cooperativeness of its members made survival possible--it was not an advantageous individual here and there who did so, but the group. In human societies the individuals who are most likely to survive are those who are best enabled to do so by their group.

Ashley Montagu, 1965

How the students perceive each other and interact with one another is a neglected aspect of instruction. Much training time is devoted to helping teachers arrange appropriate interactions between students and materials (i.e., textbooks, curriculum programs, etc.), and some time is spent on how teachers should interact with students, but how students should interact with one another is relatively ignored. It shouldn't be. How teachers structure student-student interaction patterns will have a lot to say about how well the students learn, how they feel about school and the teacher or professor, how they feel about each other, and their self-esteem.

There are three basic ways students can interact with each other as they learn. They can compete to see who is "best"; they can work individualistically on their own toward a goal without paying attention to other students, or they can work cooperatively with a vested interest in each other's learning as well as their own. Of the three interaction patterns, competition is presently the most dominant. The research indicates that a vast majority of students in the United States view school as a competitive enterprise where you try to do better than the other students. This competitive expectation is already fairly widespread when students enter school and grows stronger as they progress through school (Johnson & Johnson, 1987a). In the last 15 years, the individualistic interaction pattern has been the most talked about but has never really caught on. Cooperation among students where they cele-

brate each other's successes, encourage each other to do homework, and learn to work together regardless of ethnic backgrounds, male or female, bright or struggling, handicapped or not, is rare.

Basic Definitions

Even though these three interaction patterns are not equally effective in helping students learn concepts and skills, it is important that students learn to interact effectively in each of these patterns. Students will face situations where all three interaction patterns are operating, and they will need to be able to be effective in each situation. They also should be able to select an appropriate interaction pattern suited to the situation. An interpersonal, competitive situation is characterized by negative goal interdependence, where, when one person wins, the others lose. Do you remember the Spelling Bee where you spelled each other down or raced others to get the correct answers on the blackboard for a math problem? In an individualistic learning situation, students are independent of one another and are working toward a set criteria where their success depends on their own performance in relation to an established criteria. The success or failure of other students does not affect their score. In spelling if all students are working on their own and any student who correctly spells 90% or more words passes, it would be an individualistic structure. In a cooperative learning situation, interaction is characterized by positive goal interdependence with individual accountability. Positive goal interdependence requires acceptance by a group that they "sink or swim together." A cooperative spelling class is one where students are working together in small groups to help each other learn the words in order to take the spelling test individually on Friday. Each student's score in the test is increased by bonus points earned by the group. In that situation a student needs to be concerned with how she or he spells and how well the other students in his or her group spell. This cooperative umbrella can also be extended over the entire class if bonus points are awarded to each student when the class can spell more words than a reasonable, but demanding, criteria set by the teacher.

There is a difference between "having students work in a group" and structuring students to work cooperatively. A group of students sitting at the same table doing their own work, but free to talk with each other as they work is not structured to be a cooperative group as there is no positive interdependence. Perhaps it could be called individualistic learning with talking. There needs to be an accepted common goal on which the group will be rewarded for their efforts. In the same way, a group of students who has been assigned to do a report where only one student cares, does all the work and the others go along for a free ride, is not a cooperative group. A cooperative group has a sense of individual accountability that means that all students need to know the material or spell well for the group to be successful. Putting students into groups does not necessarily gain positive interdependence and/or individual accountability; it has to be structured and managed by the teacher or professor.

The Research Suggests . . .

When examining the research comparing students learning cooperatively, competitively, and individualistically, a very interesting paradox develops. Common practice in schools today has teachers striving to separate students from one another and have them work on their own.

Teachers continually use phrases like *Don't look at each other's papers!* or *I want to see what you can do, not your neighbor!* or *Work on your own!* Having students work alone competing with one another for grades or working on their own to reach a set criteria are the dominant interaction patterns among students in classrooms today. The paradox

is that the vast majority of the research comparing student-student interaction patterns indicates that students learn more effectively when they
work cooperatively (Johnson, 1980; Johnson & Johnson, 1987a, 1987b;
Johnson et al., 1981). The data suggest:

1. Students achieve more in cooperative interaction than in competitive
    or individualistic interaction. With several colleagues, we recently
    did a meta-analysis on all the research studies that compare coopera-
    tion, competition and individualistic learning (122 studies from 1924
    to 1980). The results indicated that cooperation seems to be much
    more powerful in producing achievement than the other interaction pat-
    terns and the results hold for several subject areas and a range of
    age groups from elementary school through adult (Johnson et al.,
    1981).

2. Students are more positive about school, subject areas, and teachers
    or professors when they are structured to work cooperatively (Johnson,
    1980; Johnson and Johnson, 1987a).

3. Students are more positive about each
    other when they learn cooperatively
    than when they learn alone, competi-
    tively, or individualistically --
    regardless of differences in ability,
    ethnic background, handicapped or not

    Johnson, 1980; Johnson & Johnson, 1986; Johnson & Johnson, 1987a).

4. Students are more effective interpersonally as a result of working
    cooperatively than when they work alone, competitively or individual-

istically.   Students with cooperative experiences are more able to
take the perspective of others, are more positive about taking part
in controversy, have better developed interaction skills, and have
a more positive expectation about working with others than students
from competitive or individualistic settings (Johnson, 1980; Johnson
& Johnson, 1979, 1987a).

With all the data that is available in this area (we now have collected
over 500 studies), it is surprising that practice in classrooms is not
more consistent with research findings.

Back to the Basics

Our research and the research of many others has established that
having students work together cooperatively is a powerful way for them
to learn and has positive effects on the classroom climate.   This has
been verified by teachers in classrooms from pre-school through graduate
school.   However, the importance of emphasizing cooperative learning
groups in classrooms goes beyond achievement, acceptance of differences,
and positive attitudes.   The ability of all students to learn to work
cooperatively with others is the keystone to building and maintaining
stable marriages, families, careers, and friendships.   Being able to perform technical skills such as reading, speaking, listening, writing, com-
puting, problem solving, etc., are valuable but of little use if the person cannot apply those skills in cooperative interaction with other
people in career, family, and community settings.   The most logical way
to emphasize the use of student's knowledge and skills within a coopera-

tive framework, such as they will meet as members of society, is to spend much of the time learning those skills in cooperative relationships with each other. We need to get back to the basics, reconcile school practice with current research, and encourage a healthy portion of instruction to be cooperative.

AUTHOR'S NOTE

We know something about interacting. In the first place we are brothers about a year and one-half apart in age, from a family of seven children growing up on a farm in Indiana. We have always been interested in people and how they interact with one another. We have had to be. Since 1972, shortly after we were brought back together from the east and west coasts to become part of the College of Education faculty, we have set aside our battles over who "sat by the window in the car last" and worked cooperatively. We became very involved in examining student-student interaction in the classroom and what effects different interaction patterns have on classroom environment and learning. Since one of us had a background in public school teaching with a high interest in instruction, and the other is a social psychologist with interest in social interactions and their effects, it was a natural collaboration, not only because we shared the same parents, but also because of our complementary academic backgrounds.

REFERENCES

Johnson, D. W. (1980). Group processes: Influences of student-student interaction on school outcomes. In J. McMillan (Ed.), **The social psychology of school learning** (123-168). New York: Academic Press.

Johnson, D. W., & Johnson, R. T. (1979). Type of task and student achievement and attitudes in interpersonal cooperation, competition, and individualization. **Journal of Social Psychology**, 108, 37-48.

Johnson, D. W., & Johnson, R. T. (1986). Impact of classroom organization and instructional methods on the effectiveness of mainstreaming. In C. Meisel (Ed.), **Mainstreaming handicapped children: Outcomes, controversies, and new directions**. Hillsdale, NJ: Lawrence Erlbaum.

Johnson, D. W., & Johnson, R. T. (1987a). **Learning together and alone: Cooperative, competitive, and individualistic learning** (2nd ed.). Englewood Cliffs, NJ: Prentice-Hall.

Johnson, D. W., & Johnson, R. T. (1987b). **A meta-analysis of cooperative, competitive, and individualistic goal structures**. Hillsdale, NJ: Lawrence Erlbaum.

Johnson, D. W., Maruyama, G., Johnson, R., Nelson, D., & Skon, L. (1981). Effects of cooperative, competitive, and individualistic goal structures on achievement: A meta-analysis. **Psychological Bulletin**, 89, 47-62.

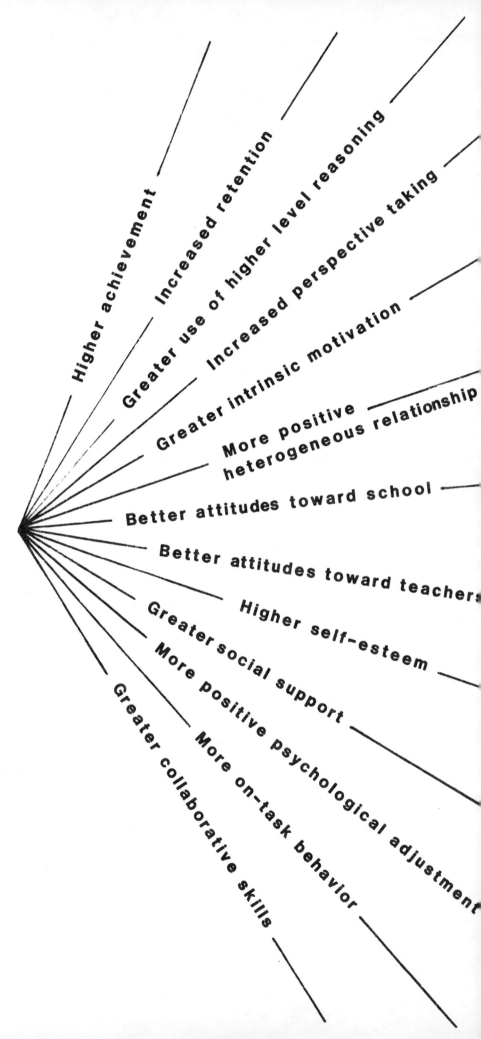

RESEARCH REVIEW

- Higher achievement
- Increased retention
- Greater use of higher level reasoning
- Increased perspective taking
- Greater intrinsic motivation
- More positive heterogeneous relationship
- Better attitudes toward school
- Better attitudes toward teachers
- Higher self-esteem
- Greater social support
- More positive psychological adjustment
- More on-task behavior
- Greater collaborative skills

Implementing Cooperative Learning: The Teachers' Role

David W. Johnson and Roger T. Johnson

University of Minnesota

What do teachers need to know in order to use cooperative learning groups effectively? One thing is clear. A prepackaged program will not work. Good teachers would feel too constricted, and average teachers would use it for a while and then drop it. What is needed is a general procedure, specific enough to give teachers guidance, but flexible enough for teachers to adapt it to their specific teaching situations.

The essence of cooperative learning is positive interdependence-- students recognize that we are in this together, sink or swim. In addition, cooperative learning situations are characterized by individual accountability, where every student is accountable for both learning the assigned material and helping other group members learn; face-to-face interaction among students; and students appropriately using interpersonal and group skills.

There is more to the teacher's role in structuring cooperative learning situations, however, than structuring cooperation among students. The teacher's role includes five major sets of strategies:

1. Clearly specifying the objectives for the lesson.

2. Making decisions about placing students in learning groups before the lesson is taught.

3. Clearly explaining the task, goal structure, and learning activity to the students.

4. Monitoring the effectiveness of the cooperative learning
    groups and intervening to provide task assistance (such as
    answering questions and teaching task skills) or to increase
    students' interpersonal and group skills.

5. Evaluating students' achievement and helping students dis-
    cuss how well they collaborated with each other.

The following 18 steps elaborate these strategies and detail a procedure for structuring cooperative learning. Specific examples of lessons may be found in this handbook. There are also two films available
demonstrating the use of cooperative learning procedures (Belonging,
Circles of Learning).

OBJECTIVES

1. Specifying Instructional Objectives

There are two types of objectives that a teacher needs to specify
before the lesson begins. The **academic objective** needs to be specified
at the correct level for the students and matched to the right level of
instruction according to a conceptual or task analysis. The **collaborative skills objective** details what collaborative skills are going to be
emphasized during the lesson.

DECISIONS

2. Deciding on the Size of the Group

Once the lesson objectives are clear, the teacher must decide which
size of learning group is optimal. Cooperative learning groups tend to
range in size from two to six. A number of factors should be

considered in selecting the size of a cooperative learning group:

a. As the size of the group increases, the range of abilities, expertise, skills, and number of minds available for acquiring and processing information increase. The more group members you have, the more chance to have someone who has special knowledge helpful to the group and the more willing hands and talents are available to do the task.

b. The larger the group, however, the more skillful group members must be in providing everyone with a chance to speak, coordinating the actions of group members, reaching consensus, ensuring elaboration of the material being learned, and keeping all members on task. Very few students have the collaborative skills needed for effective group functioning and, therefore, the skills have to be initially taught.

c. The materials available or the specific nature of the task may dictate group size.

d. The shorter the period of time available, the smaller the learning group should be. Smaller groups will be more effective because they take less time to get organized, they operate faster, and there is more "air time" per member.

Our best advice to beginning teachers is to start with pairs or threesomes. As students become more experienced and skillful, they will be able to manage larger groups. Six may be the upper limit for a cooperative learning group in most schools--more members would be too large even for **very** skillful members. In one classroom we recently observed the teacher had divided the class into "committees" of eight. In the typical committee some students were being left out, others were passive, and some were engaged in a conversation with only one or two other members. Cooperative learning groups need to be small enough for everyone to engage in mutual discussion while achieving the group's goals. So be cautious about group size. Some students will not be ready for a group as large as four.

3. **Assigning Students to Groups**

There are five basic questions teachers often ask about assigning students to groups:

a. Should students be placed in learning groups homogeneous or heterogeneous in member ability? There are times when cooperative homogeneous learning groups may be used to master specific skills or to achieve certain instructional objectives. Generally, however, we recommend that teachers emphasize heterogeneity of students--placing high-, medium-, and low-ability students within the same learning group. More elaborative thinking, more frequent giving and receiving of explanations, and greater perspective in discussing material seem to occur in heterogeneous groups, all of which increase the depth of understanding, the quality of reasoning, and the accuracy of long-term retention.

b. Should non-task-oriented students be placed in learning groups with task-oriented peers or be separated? To keep such students on task, it often helps to place them in a cooperative learning group with task-oriented peers.

c. Should students select who they want to work with or should the teacher assign groups? Having students select their own groups is often not very successful. Student-selected groups often are homogeneous with high-achieving students working with other high-achieving students, white students working with other white students, minority students working with other minority students, and males working with other males. Often there is less on-task behavior in student-selected than in teacher-selected groups. A useful modification of the select your own group method is to have students list who they would like to work with and then place them in a learning group with one person they chose plus a few more students selected by the teacher. Teacher-made groups often have the best mix since teachers can put together optimal combinations of students. There are many ways teachers may assign students to learning groups. Some additional ways are:

1. Ask students to list three peers with whom they would like to work. Identify the isolated students who are not chosen by any other classmates. Then build a group of skillful and supportive students around each isolated child.

2. Randomly assign students by having them count off and placing the one's together, the two's together, and so forth. If groups of three are desired in a class of 30, have the students count off by tens.

3. How do desegregation and mainstreaming relate to how teachers assign students to learning groups? In order to build constructive relationships between majority and minority students, between handicapped and nonhandicapped students, and even between male and female students, use heterogeneous cooperative learning groups with a variety of students within each learning group.

d. How long should the groups stay together? For the length of the instructional unit? Actually, there is no formula or simple answer to this question. Some teachers keep cooperative learning groups together for an entire year or semester. Other teachers change group membership often. An elementary school setting allows students to be in several different learning groups during the day. Our best advice is to allow groups to remain stable long enough for them to be successful. Breaking up groups that are having trouble functioning effectively is often counterproductive, as the students do not learn the skills they need to resolve problems in collaborating with each other.

There is merit in having students work with everyone in their class during a semester or school year. Building a strong positive feeling of collaboration across an entire class and giving students opportunities to practice the skills needed to begin new groups can add much to the learning experience. Finally, never underestimate the power of heterogenous cooperative learning groups in promoting high quality, rich and involved learning.

4. Arranging the Room

How the teacher arranges the room is a symbolic message of what is appropriate behavior, and it can facilitate the learning groups within the classroom. The group members should sit in a circle and be close enough to each other to communicate effectively without disrupting the other learning groups, and the teacher should have a clear access lane to every group.

One common mistake that teachers make in arranging a room is to place students at a rectangular table where they cannot have eye contact with all the other members; another is to place a number of desks together, which places students too far apart to quietly communicate with each other. Within each learning group students need to be able to see all relevant task materials, see each other, converse with each other without raising their voices, and exchange ideas and materials in a comfortable atmosphere. The groups need to be far enough apart so that they do not interfere with each other's learning.

5. Planning the Instructional Materials to Promote Interdependence

The way teachers structure the materials to be used during a lesson can lead both to effective academic learning and positive interdependence among group members. When a group is mature and experienced and group members have a high level of collaborative skills, the teacher may not have to arrange materials in any specific way. When a group is new or when members are not very skilled, however, teachers may wish to distribute materials in carefully planned ways to communicate that the assignment is to be a joint (not an individual) effort and that the students are in a **sink** **or** **swim** **together** learning situation. Three ways of doing so are:

a. **Materials Interdependence:** Give only one copy of the materials to the group. The students will then have to work together in order to be successful. This is especially effective the first few times the group meets. After students are accustomed to collaborating with each other, teachers will wish each student to have an individual copy of the materials.

b. **Information Interdependence:** Group members may each be given different books or resource materials to be synthesized. Or the materials may be arranged like a jigsaw puzzle so that each student has part of the materials needed to complete the task (Aronson, and others, 1978). Such pro-cedures require that every member participate in order for the group to be successful.

c. **Interdependence with Other Groups:** Materials may be structured into a tournament format with intergroup competition as the basis to promote a perception of interdependence among group members. Such a procedure was introduced by DeVries and Edwards (1973) and extended by Slavin (1974). In the teams-games-tournament format, students are divided into heterogene-ous cooperative learning teams to prepare members for a tourna-ment in which they compete with the other teams. During the in-tergroup competition the students individually compete against members of about the same ability level from other teams. The team whose members do the best in the competition is pronounced the winner.

All of these procedures may not be needed simultaneously. They are alternative methods of ensuring that students perceive that they must work together and behave collaboratively to succeed in the learning situation.

6. Assigning Roles to Ensure Interdependence

Cooperative interdependence may also be arranged through the assignment of complementary and interconnected roles to group members. An example is a science lesson we helped develop. Each group member is assigned a responsibility that must be fulfilled if the group is to function. For example, the group should have a **summarizer-checker** to make sure everyone in the group understands what is being learned; a **researcher-runner** to get needed materials for the group and to communicate with the other learning groups and the teacher; a **recorder** to write down the group's decisions and to edit the group's report; an **encourager**

ENCOURAGER

to reinforce members' contributions; and an **observer** to keep track of how well the group is collaborating. Assigning such roles is an effective method of teaching students collaborative skills.

With these decisions made and the appropriate materials prepared, the teacher is ready to explain the instructional task and the cooperative goal structure to the class. The less experience the students have in working in cooperative learning groups, the more important it is that teachers explain carefully what cooperation is.

TASK, GOAL STRUCTURE, LEARNING ACTIVITY

7. Explaining the Academic Task

Teachers should consider several aspects of explaining an academic assignment to students:

a. Set the task so that students are clear about the assignment. Most teachers have considerable practice with this. Instructions that are clear and specific are crucial in warding off student frustration. One advantage of cooperative learning groups is that these students can handle more ambiguous tasks (when appropriate) than can students working alone. In cooperative learning groups students who do not understand what they are to do will ask their group for clarification before asking the teacher.

b. Explain the objectives of the lesson and relate the concepts and information to be studied to students' past experience and learning to ensure maximum transfer and retention. Explaining the intended outcomes of the lesson increases the likelihood that students will focus on the relevant concepts and information throughout the lesson.

c. Define relevant concepts, explain procedures students should follow, and give examples to help students understand what they are to learn and to do in completing the assignment. To promote positive transfer of learning, point out the critical elements that separate this lesson from past learnings.

d. Ask the class specific questions to check the students' understanding of the assignment. Such questioning ensures that thorough two-way communication exists, that the assignment has been given effectively, and that the students are ready to begin completing it.

8. Structuring Positive Goal Interdependence

Communicate to students that they have a group goal and must work collaboratively. We cannot overemphasize the importance of communicating to students that they are in a **sink or swim together** learning situation. In a cooperative learning group students must understand that they are responsible for learning the assigned material, making sure that all other group members learn the assigned material, and making sure that all other group members successfully complete the assignments, in that order. Teachers can do this in several ways:

a. Ask the group to produce a single product, report, or paper. Each group member should sign the paper to indicate that he or she agrees with the answers and can explain why the answers are appropriate. Each student must know the material. When a group is producing only one product it is especially important to stress individual accountability. Teachers may pick a student at random from each group to explain the rationale for their answers.

b. Provide group rewards. A group grade is one way to emphasize the necessity for collaboration. A spelling group where the group members work with each other during the week to make sure that all members know their words, so they can take the test individually, can be rewarded on the basis of the total number of words spelled correctly by all the members of the group. Math lessons can be structured so that students work in cooperative learning groups, take a test individually, receive an individual score, but are given bonus points on the basis of how many group members reach a preset level of excellence. Some teachers reward groups where all members reach a preset criterion of excellence with free-time or extra recess.

Positive interdependence creates peer encouragement and support for learning. Such positive peer pressure influences under-achieving students to become academically involved. Members of cooperative learning groups should give two interrelated messages: "Do your work--we're counting on you!" and "How can I help you to do better?"

9. Structuring Individual Accountability

The purpose of a cooperative learning group is to enhance the learning of each member. A learning group is not truly cooperative if individual members let others do all the work. In order to ensure that all members learn and that groups know which members to provide with encouragement and help, teachers will need to assess frequently the level of performance of each group member--by giving practice tests, randomly selecting members to explain answers, having members edit each other's work, or by randomly picking one paper from the group to grade. These are only a few ways individual accountability can be structured.

10. Structuring Intergroup Cooperation

The positive outcomes found within a cooperative learning group can be extended throughout a whole class by structuring intergroup cooperation other than through the competitive tournament format. Bonus points may be given if all members of a class reach a preset criterion of excellence. When a group finishes its work, the teacher should encourage the members to help other groups complete the assignment.

11. Explaining Criteria for Success

Rather than grading on a curve, evaluation within cooperatively structured lessons needs to be based on criteria established for acceptable work. Thus, at the beginning of the lesson teachers should clearly explain the criteria by which the students' work will be evaluated. The criteria for success must be structured so that students may reach it without penalizing other students and so that groups may reach it without penalizing other groups.

For some learning groups, all members can be working to reach the same criteria. For other learning groups, different members may be evaluated according to different criteria. The criteria should be tailored to be challenging and realistic for each individual group member. In a spelling group, for example, some members may not be able to learn as many as 20 words, and the number of words for such students can be reduced accordingly.

Teachers may structure a second level of cooperation not only by keeping track of how well each group and its members are performing, but also by setting criteria for the whole class to reach. Thus, the number of words the total class spells correctly can be recorded from week to week with appropriate criteria being set to promote class-wide collaboration and encouragement.   These criteria are important to give students information about what "doing well" means on assigned tasks, but they do not always have to be as formal as counting the number of correct answers.   On some assignments, simply completing the task may be an adequate criterion for assessing the work of some students.   For others, simply doing better this week than last week may be set as a criterion of excellence.

12. Specifying Desired Behaviors

The word cooperation has different connotations and uses.   Teachers need to define cooperation operationally by specifying the behaviors that are appropriate and desirable within the learning groups.   There are beginning behaviors, such as "stay with your group and do not wander around the room," "use quiet voices," "take turns," and "use each other's names."   When groups begin to function more effectively, expected behaviors may include:

a. Have each member explain how to get the answer.

b. Ask each member to relate what is being learned to previous learnings.

c. Check to make sure everyone in the group understands the material and agrees with the answers the group has developed.

d. Encourage everyone to participate.

e. Listen accurately to what all group members are saying.

f. Encourage each member to be persuaded by the logic of the answers proposed, not by group pressure; majority rule does not promote learning.

g. Criticize ideas, not people.

The list of expected behaviors should not be too long. One or two behaviors is enough for a few lessons. Students need to know what behavior is appropriate and desirable within a cooperative learning group, but they should not be subjected to information overload.

MONITORING AND INTERVENING

13. Monitoring Students' Behavior

The teacher's job begins in earnest when the cooperative learning groups start working. Resist that urge to get a cup of coffee or grade some papers. Just because the teacher places students in learning groups and instructs them to be cooperative does not mean that they will always do so. Therefore, much of the teacher's time should be spent in observing group members in order to see what problems they are having in completing the assignment and in working collaboratively. A variety of observation instruments and procedures that can be used for these purposes can be found in Johnson and Johnson (1984, 1987) and Johnson and F. Johnson (1987).

Whenever possible, teachers should use a formal observation sheet to count the number of times they observe appropriate behaviors being used by students. The more concrete the data, the more useful it is to the teacher and to students. Teachers should not try to count too many different behaviors at one time, especially when they start formal observation. At first they may just record who talks in each group to

get a participation pattern for the groups. Some help on
observation can be found in a chapter describing systema-
tic observation of cooperative groups in **Learning
Together and Alone** (Johnson and Johnson, 1987). Our current list of behaviors (though rather long) includes: contributing
ideas, asking questions, expressing feelings, actively listening, expressing support and acceptance (toward ideas), expressing warmth and
liking (toward group members and group), encouraging all members to participate, summarizing, checking for understanding, relieving tension by
joking, and giving direction to the group work.

We look for positive behaviors, which are to be praised when they
are appropriately present and which are a cause for discussion when they
are missing. It is also a good idea for the teacher to collect notes
on specific student behaviors so that the frequency data is extended.
Especially useful are skillful interchanges that can be shared with students later in the form of objective praise and perhaps with parents in
conferences or telephone conversations.

Student observers can get even more extensive data on each group's
functioning. For very young students the system must be kept very
simple, perhaps only "Who talks?" Many teachers have had success with
student observers, even in kindergarten.

One of the more important things the teacher can do is to make sure
that the class is given adequate instructions (and perhaps practice) on
gathering the observation data and sharing it with the group. The observer is in the best position to learn about the skills of working in

a group. We remember one 1st-grade teacher who had a student who talked all the time (even to himself while working alone). He dominated any group he was in. When the teacher introduced student observers to the class, she made the student an observer. (One important rule for observers is not to interfere in the task but to gather data without talking.) He gathered data on who talked and did a good job, noting that one student had done quite a bit of talking in the group while another had talked very little. The next day when he was back in the group and no longer the observer, he started to talk, clamped his hand over his mouth, and glanced at the new observer. He knew what behavior was being observed, and he didn't want to be the only one with marks for talking. The teacher said he may have listened for the first time all year. Thus the observer often benefits by learning about group skills.

Observers, moreover, often know quite a bit about the lesson. When teachers are worried about losing the lesson content, they can have the observer take the group through the material as a last review. Often important changes are made during this review.

It is not necessary to use student observers all the time, and we would not recommend their use until cooperative learning groups have been used a few times. In the beginning it is enough for teachers simply to structure the groups to be cooperative without worrying about structuring student observers, too. Whether student observers are used or not, however, teachers should always do some observing and spend time monitoring the groups. Sometimes a simple checklist is helpful in addition to a systematic observation form. Some questions to ask on the checklist might be: Are students practicing the specified behaviors, or

not?   Do they understand the task?   Have they accepted the positive
interdependence and the individual accountability?   Are they working toward the criteria and are the criteria for success appropriate?

14. Providing Task Assistance

In monitoring the groups as they work, teachers will wish to clarify instructions, review important procedures and strategies for completing the assignment, answer questions, and teach task skills as necessary.   In discussing the concepts and information to be learned,
teachers should use the language or terms relevant to the learning.   Instead of saying, "Yes, that is right," teachers might say something more
specific to the assignment, such as, "Yes, that is one way to find the
main idea of a paragraph."   The use of specific statements reinforces
the desired learning and promotes positive transfer.

15. Intervening to Teach Collaborative Skills

While monitoring the learning groups, teachers sometimes find students without the necessary collaborative skills and groups with problems in collaborating.   In these cases the teacher may intervene to suggest more effective procedures for working together and more effective
behaviors for students to engage in.   Teachers may also wish to intervene and reinforce particularly effective and skillful behaviors as they
are noticed.   The teacher at times is a consultant to a group.   When it
is obvious that group members lack the necessary collaborative skills
to cooperate with each other, the coordinator will want to intervene to
help the members learn these skills.   Collaborative skills, along with

activities that may be used in teaching them, are covered in Johnson and Johnson (1987) and Johnson (1986, 1987).

Teachers should not intervene in the groups any more than is absolutely necessary. Most teachers are geared to jumping in and solving problems for students as they occur. With a little patience, we find that cooperative groups can often work their way through their own problems (task and maintenance) and acquire not only a solution, but also a method of solving similar problems in the future. Choosing when to intervene and when not to is part of the art of teaching, and teachers can usually trust their intuition. Even after intervening, teachers can turn the problem back to the group to solve. Many teachers intervene by having members set aside their task, pointing out the problem, and asking the group to come up with an adequate solution. The last thing teachers want is for the students to come running to the teacher with every problem.

For example, a 3rd-grade teacher noticed while passing out papers that one student was leaning back away from the other three group members. A moment later, the three students marched over to the teacher and complained that Johnny was under the table and wouldn't come out. "Make him come out!" they insisted (the teacher's role: police officer, judge, and executioner). The teacher told them that Johnny was a member of their group and asked what they had tried. The children were puzzled. "Yes, have you asked him to come out?" the teacher suggested. The group marched back, and the teacher continued passing out papers. A moment later, the teacher glanced at their table and saw no heads above the table (which is one way to solve the problem). Shortly, four heads came struggling out from under the table, and the group (including Johnny) went back to work with great energy.

We don't know what happened under that table, but whatever it was, it was effective. What makes this story even more interesting is that the group received a 100 percent on the paper and later, when the teacher was at Johnny's desk, she noticed he had the paper clutched in his hand. The group had given Johnny the paper and he was taking it home. He confided to the teacher that this was the first time he could ever remember earning a 100 percent on anything in school. (If that was **your** record, you might slip under a few tables yourself.)

The best time to teach cooperative skills is when the students need them. It is important that the cooperative skills be taught in the appropriate context, or are practiced in that setting, because transfer of skill learning from one situation to another cannot be assumed. Students **learn about** cooperative skills when they are taught them, and **learn** cooperative skills when applying them in science, math, or English. The good news about cooperative skills is that they are taught and learned like any other skill. At a minimum:

a. Students need to recognize the need for the skill.

b. The skill must be defined clearly and specifically including what students should say when engaging in the skill.

c. Practice of the skill must be encouraged. Sometimes just the teacher standing nearby with a clipboard and pencil will be enough to promote student enactment of the skill.

d. Students should have the time and procedures to discuss how
    well they are using the skill.

e. Students should persevere in the practice until the skill is
    appropriately internalized. We never drop a skill, we only add
    on.

For older students (upper elementary school and above) the skills
have been worked out and summarized in **Joining Together** (Johnson and F.
Johnson, 1987) and **Reaching Out** (Johnson, 1986). For younger students,
teachers may need to revise and rename cooperative skills. Some primary
teachers use symbols like traffic signs with a "green light" encouraging participation, a "stop sign" meaning time to summarize,
and "slippery when wet" meaning "Say that over again; I
didn't quite understand."

Sometimes a more mechanistic structure is beneficial for young students.   In one 1st-grade class, there were a number of students who
liked to dominate and take over the group. One day, in frustration, the
teacher formed groups and handed each group member five poker chips with
a different color for each group member. The students were instructed
to place one chip in a box every time they spoke while working on the

worksheet.   A student could not speak after all his or her
chips were "spent." When all the chips were in the box, they
could get their five colored chips back and start again.
Several students were surprised when they discovered their five
chips were the only ones in the box!

Teachers need only use these devices once or twice to get the message across. This technique was later used in a monthly principals' meeting. As the principals came in, each was handed several colored strips of paper. When they spoke . . .

Teaching cooperative skills is necessary for implementing cooperative learning groups into a classroom. We recommended that only a few skills be taught each semester. Most curriculum programs with cooperative learning groups written into them feature about five to eight cooperative skills for one year.

16. Providing Content Closure to the Lesson

At the end of the lesson, students should be able to summarize what they have learned and to understand where they will use it in future lessons. To reinforce student learning, teachers may wish to summarize the major points in the lesson, ask students to recall ideas or give samples, and answer any final questions they may have.

EVALUATING AND PROCESSING

17. Evaluating the Quality of Students' Learning

The product required from the lesson may be a report, a single set of answers agreed upon by all group members, the average of individual examination scores, or the number of group members reaching a specific criterion. As we pointed out earlier, whatever the product, student learning needs to be evaluated by a criteria-referenced system. The procedures for setting up and using such an evaluation system are given in Johnson and Johnson (1987). In addition to an assessment on how well they are learning the assigned concepts and information, group members should also receive feedback on how effectively they collaborated. Some teachers give two grades, one for achievement and one for collaborative behavior.

18. Assessing How Well the Group Functioned

An old rule concerning observations of groups states that if you observe, you also must process those observations with the group. Processing need not occur in depth every day, but should happen often. Even if class time is limited, some time should be spent talking about how well the groups functioned today, what things were done well, and what things could be improved. Whole-class processing can include some feedback from the teacher (the principal observer) and some observations from members of the class. This can often include having a group share with the class an incident in their group and how they solved it. Names need not be used, but the feedback should be as specific as possible.

Groups new to processing often need an agenda, including specific questions each group member must address. A simple agenda might request each group to name two things they did well (and document them) and one thing they need to do even better, or would like to work harder on.

The time spent in discussing how well the group functioned is well spent, since each small group has two primary goals: (a) to accomplish the task successfully, and (b) to build and maintain constructive relationships in good working order for the next task. If a group is growing properly, it will become more and more effective. Often during the "working" part of the class period, students will be very task-oriented, and the "maintenance" of the group may suffer. During the processing time, however, the emphasis is on maintenance of the group, and the students leave the room ready for (a better?) tomorrow. If no processing is done, teachers may find the group's functioning decaying, and important relationships left undiscussed. Processing the functioning of the group needs to be taken as seriously as accomplishing the task. The two are very much related. Teachers often have students turn in a "process sheet" along with the paper required from the task assignment. Teachers will want to have a structured agenda or checklist for the groups to work with during the processing as inexperienced groups tend to say, "We did fine. Right? Right!" and not deal with any relevant issues.

Group processing should focus both on members' contributions to each other's learning and to the maintenance of effective working relationships among group members. In order to contribute to each other's learning, group members need to attend class, to have completed the necessary homework required for the group's work, and to have provided needed explanations and examples. Absenteeism and lack of preparation often demoralize other members. A productive group discussion is one in which members are present and prepared and there should be some peer accountability to be so.

On the other hand, learning groups are often exclusively task oriented and ignore the importance of maintaining effective working relationships among members. Group sessions should be enjoyable, lively and pleasant. If no one is having fun, something is wrong. Problems should be brought up and solved, and there should be a continuing emphasis on improving the effectiveness of the group members in collaborating with each other.

CONCLUSIONS

These 18 aspects of structuring learning situations cooperatively blend together to make effective cooperative learning groups a reality in the classroom. They may be used in any subject area with any age student. Teachers who have mastered these strategies and integrated cooperative learning groups into their teaching often say, "Don't say it is easy!" There is a lot of pressure to teach like everyone else is teaching, to have students learn alone, and to not let students look on each other's papers. Students will not be accustomed to working together and are likely to have a competitive orientation. It isn't easy, but it is worth the effort.

Another bit of advice would be to start small and build. Pick a time in the school day when you are pretty sure it would work, plan carefully, and don't rush the process. Cooperative learning groups should evolve into a teacher's program rather than to become a part of every class on the first day.

The good news is that many of your students will do well immediately. While two groups may struggle because of a lack of group skills, five will do well. Celebrate the five and problem solve with the two. Keep in mind that the students who are most difficult to integrate into groups are often the ones who need the peer support and positive peer pressure the most. Resist that advice you were given as a beginning teacher to isolate students who pester others or show that they lack interpersonal skills; instead, concentrate on integrating them into their peer group effectively. Other students often have the most powerful influence on isolated, alienated students. Such students cannot be allowed to plod through school disconnected, lonely, and bitter.

In addition, cooperative, supportive relationships are just as productive for adults as they are for students. Teachers are more effective when they have positive support from colleagues and can solve problems together. Teachers need to give some thought to establishing their own cooperative group as they implement cooperation in their classrooms.

It is also important to repeat that we would be disappointed if we visited a teacher's classroom and saw only cooperative learning groups. The data are clear. Cooperation should produce better results in school than having student work alone, individualistically or competitively. Yet there is an important place for competitive and individualistic goal structures within the classroom. The major problems with competition and individualistic efforts result from overuse or inappropriate use.

In addition to cooperative skills, students need to learn how to compete for fun and enjoyment (win or lose) and how to work independently, following through on a task until completion. The natural place for competitive and individualistic efforts is under the umbrella of cooperation. The predominant use of cooperation reduces the anxiety and evaluation apprehension associated with competition. It also allows for using individualistically structured learning activities as part of a

division of labor within cooperative tasks. But, most of all, students
should learn how to work together and to give each other support in
learning. Some teachers weave the three goal structures together: setting up individual responsibility (accountability to the group), peer
teaching, competing as a light change of pace, and ending in a cooperative project. Thus, they do what schools should do--prepare students
to interact effectively in cooperative, competitive, and individualistic
structures.

REFERENCES

Aronson, E., Blaney, N., Stephan, C., Sikes, J., & Snapp, M. (1968). The jigsaw classroom. Beverly Hills, CA: Sage Publications.

DeVries, D., & Edwards, K. (1973). Learning games and student teams: Their effects on classroom process. American Educational Research Journal, 10, 307–318.

Johnson, D. W. (1986). Reaching out: Interpersonal effectiveness and self-actualization (3rd ed.). Englewood Cliffs, NJ: Prentice-Hall.

Johnson, D. W. (1987). Human relations and your career (2nd ed.). Englewood Cliffs, NJ: Prentice-Hall.

Johnson, D. W., & Johnson, F. (1987). Joining together: Group theory and group skills. Englewood Cliffs, NJ: Prentice-Hall.

Johnson, D. W., & Johnson, R. T. (1984). Cooperation in the classroom. Edina, MN: Interaction Book Company.

Johnson, D. W., & Johnson, R. T. (1987). Learning together and alone: Cooperative, competitive, and individualistic learning (2nd ed.). Englewood Cliffs, NJ: Prentice-Hall.

Slavin, R. (1974). The effects of teams in Teams-Games-Tournament on the normative climates of classrooms. Technical report, Center for Social Organization of Schools, Johns Hopkins University.

Teacher's Role

Decisions

Size of Group

Assigning Students

Arranging the Room

Planning the Materials

Assigning Roles

Monitoring and Intervening

Providing Task Assistance

Monitoring Student Behavior

Intervening

Closure to Lesson

Setting Task & Positive Interdependence

Explaining Task

Structuring Positive Goal Interdependence

Structuring Individual Accountability

Structuring Intergroup Cooperation

Explaining Criteria for Success

Specifying Desired Behaviors

Evaluating and Processing

Evaluating the Quantity and Quality of Student's Learning

Assessing Group Functioning

Getting Started with Cooperative Groups

David W. Johnson, Roger T. Johnson and Edythe Johnson Holubec

To begin using cooperative learning groups there are a number of stages teachers may go through. Once a teacher has made a decision to try cooperative learning, there may be an initial rather awkward use within which the lessons may not go well because both the students and the teacher are new to a system of using cooperative groups for instructional purposes. There are a number of "start up" issues such as teaching students the cooperative skills they need to work together effectively, and training students in how to move into and out of groups quickly and quietly. Once both the teacher and the students become used to the system of cooperative learning, then a stage of mechanically using cooperative learning procedures may set in. Teachers follow the general procedures for implementing cooperative learning in a step-by-step fashion, planning each lesson, and reviewing recommended procedures before each lesson. It may take teachers a year to reach this stage. Finally, when the cooperative learning strategies are fully integrated into the teachers' repertoires, teachers reach the routine-use level in which lessons may be automatically structured for cooperative learning situations without conscious thought or planning. The concurrent focus on academic and collaborative skills takes place spontaneously. It may take teachers two years to reach this stage. Some advice that may be helpful is:

1. Do not try to move this fast. Start with a single lesson. Move to conducting at least one cooperative lesson per week and then to

 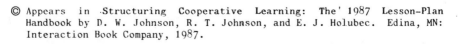

modifying a curriculum unit to be primarily cooperative.

2. Persevere!   Do not stop growing in your use of cooperative learning even though some students are not very skillful and no one else in your school seems to care. Lay out a long-range plan and stay with it. Especially persevere with students who have a hard time collaborating with peers.

3. Seek support from one or more colleagues and engage in joint sharing of successes, problems, new ideas, and curriculum modification.

4. Plan carefully for the start of each school year so that cooperative learning is emphasized right away.

Within this article practical advice is presented in order to help teachers move from the initial to routine stages of using cooperative learning strategies.

Assigning Students to Learning Groups

There are many different ways to assign students to learning groups. The following sections contain some suggestions for grouping students. For further methods, along with a number of warm-up strategies, see R. Johnson and Johnson (1985).

Stratified Random

1. Rank order students from highest to lowest in terms of a pretest on the unit, a recent past test, past grades, or your best guess as a teacher.

2. Select the first group by choosing the highest student, the

lowest student, and the two middle achievers. Assign them to the group unless they are all of one sex, they do not reflect the ethnic composition of the class, they are worst enemies, or they are best friends. If any of these are true, move up or down one student from the middle to readjust.

3. Select the remaining groups by repeating the above procedure with the reduced list. If there are students left over, make one or two groups of three members.

The same procedure may be used for assigning students to groups of three or two members.

Numbering

Divide the number of students in the class by the size of the group you wish to use (30 students divided by 3 = 10). Have students number off by the result (e.g., 10). Then have the students with the same number find each other.

Teachers may include handing out materials that have a number or symbol on them and ask students to find their classmates with the same number or symbol. Teachers may also pass out cards with a number or symbol on them to assign students to learning groups.

There are many variations to this procedure. Teachers may place a list of words on the board, such as a list of colors, animals, countries, rocks, or plants, and have students "word off." You need the same number of words as groups you wish to assign students to.

Roger's favorite variation is to count off in a different language (e.g., English, Spanish, French, Hungarian) each time students are assigned to groups. His rule is that any language may only be used one time during a semester or year.

Reducing Isolation

1. Ask students to list three peers with whom they would like to work.

2. Identify the isolated students who are not chosen by any other of their classmates.

3. Build a group of skillful and supportive students around each isolated student.

Math Method

There are endless variations to the math method of assigning students to groups. The basic structure is to give each student a math problem and ask students whose problems have the same answer to group together. This may vary from simple addition in the first grade to complex equations in high school classes. Thus, to form a group of three, the following three equations may be distributed throughout the class (3 + 3 = ; 4 + 2 = ; 5 + 1 =).

States and Capitols

To assign students to groups of two or four the following procedure may be used. Divide the number of students in the class by two (30 divided by 2 = 15). Pick a geographic area of the U.S. and write out on cards the names of 15 states. Then on another set of cards write out the names of their capitol cities. Shuffle the cards

and pass them out to students. Then have the students find the classmate
who has the matching state or capitol. To form groups of four, have two
adjacent states and their capitols combine.

Historical Characters

Give each student a card with the name of a historical character. S/he can then find the other members of their group on the basis of the historical
period in which the characters lived. Variations include grouping according to the occupation of the
person, country they came from, or significant event or accomplishment.

Geographical Areas

List a number of countries or states and have students group themselves according to most preferred to visit. Variations include grouping
according to least preferred to visit, similar in terms of climate, similar in geological features, and so forth.

Literature Characters

Give students individual cards with the names of characters in the
literature they recently have read. Ask them to group with the characters
from the same story, play, or poem. Examples include Romeo and Juliet;
Captain Hook, Peter Pan and Wendy; and Hansel, Gretel, Ginger-Bread-House
Witch, and Step-Mother.

Preferences

Have students write their favorite sport to participate in on a slip
of paper. Then have them find groupmates who like to participate in the
same sport. Variations include favorite food, celebrity, skill, car,

president, animal, vegetable, fairy tale character, and so forth.

Helpful Hints

1. Explain to the class that before the year is over, everyone will work in a group with everyone else and, therefore, if you are not in a group with someone you would like to be, do not worry about it. The next group will be different.

2. Ask the students to help ensure that the groups are heterogeneous in terms of sex, ethnicity, and ability. In order to build constructive relationships between majority and minority students, between handicapped and nonhandicapped students, and even between male and female students, use heterogeneous cooperative learning groups with a variety of students within each learning group.

3. Before the students start to move into their groups say, "I would like you to take responsibility to make sure that everyone is included in a group. Before you begin the group task, look around the room. If you see someone who is not in a group, invite them to join your group or another group that has fewer members.

Starting Up Advice

An advantage of group work is that students become more directly involved in their learning and thereby learn more and enjoy it more. Specifically, students get immediate feedback on how well they learned, teach their peers, see learning strategies modelled, and verbalize what they learn. A disadvantage of group work is that many students don't know how to work effectively in groups, so problems arise. To minimize these problems, try the following:

1. Make up the groups yourself. Each group should have a high, medium, and low-achieving student in it, with a mix of sexes, cultural groups, and motivation levels in order to be most powerful. Do not put students with their friends unless you have a good reason. If students protest their group membership, explain that you will make new groups later on, so they won't always be with the same people.

2. Seat students close to their group members. This makes it quick and easy for you to get them in and out of their groups.

3. Start out with small groups. Groups sized two or three are best until students become skillful in including everyone. Then proceed carefully to four if you wish.

4. Integrate group work into your curriculum. Anything one can do, two can do better. Have them drill each other in pairs over material taught. Review for tests in trios. On some assignments, have them do the work individually first, then decide on group answers. They can certify each other's papers for accuracy, then you can pick one paper to grade. Three students can discuss chapter questions and turn in one paper for the group. The more oral discussion and summarizing of material the students do, the more they will learn.

5. Assign each student a job or role. Possibilities include **Reader**, **Recorder**, **Checker** (makes certain everyone knows and can explain the answers by having group members summarize), **Encourager** (encourages full participation by asking silent members what they think or what they have to add), and **Praiser** (praises good ideas or helpful group members).

6. Make your expectations of group behavior clear. *I expect to see everyone staying with the group, contributing ideas, listening carefully to other group members, making certain everyone is included in the work, and making certain everyone understands and agrees.*

7. Observe and question while students are working. Ask anyone you don't think is helping to explain an answer. Make it clear to the group that it is responsible for making sure all group members participate and know the answers. Expect that some groups will finish before other groups; check over their work and have them correct any glaring errors, then let them review, talk quietly, study, or read until the other groups are finished.

8. After each session, have each group answer: *What did we do well today in working together? What could we do even better tomorrow?* Let them know what you saw them do. Be positive and reward positive behaviors.

Some Quick Cooperative Starters

Although we have found few limits to the number of ways Cooperative Learning groups can be used, here are some ideas to get you started.

1. **Turn to Your Neighbor.** Three to five minutes. Ask the students to turn to a neighbor and ask h/her something about the lesson: to explain a concept you've just taught; to explain the assignment; to explain how to do what you've just taught; to summarize the three most important points of the discussion, or whatever fits the lesson.

2. **Reading Groups.** Students read material together and answer the questions. One person is the **Reader**, another the Recorder, and the third the **Checker** (who checks to make certain everyone understands and agrees with the answers. They must come up with three possible answers to each question and circle their favorite one. When finished, they sign the paper to certify that they all understand and agree on the answers.

3. **Jigsaw.** Each person reads and studies part of a selection, then teaches what he or she has learned to the other members of the group. Each then quizzes the group members until satisfied that everyone knows his or her part thoroughly.

4. **Focus Trios.** Before a film, lecture, or reading, have students summarize together what they already know about the subject and come up with questions they have about it. Afterwards, the trios answer questions, discuss new information, and formulate new questions.

5. **Drill Partners.** Have students drill each other on the facts they need

to know until they are certain both partners know and can remember them all. This works for spelling, vocabulary, math, grammar, test review, etc. Give bonus points on the test if all members score above a certain percentage.

6. **Reading Buddies.** In lower grades, have students read their stories to each other, getting help with words and discussing content with their partners. In upper grades, have students tell about their books and read their favorite parts to each other.

7. **Worksheet Checkmates.** Have two students, each with different jobs, do one worksheet. The **Reader** reads, then suggests an answer; the **Writer** either agrees or comes up with another answer. When they both understand and agree on an answer, the **Writer** can write it.

8. **Homework Checkers.** Have students compare homework answers, discuss any they have not answered similarly, then correct their papers and add the reason they changed an answer. They make certain everyone's answers agree, then staple the papers together. You grade one paper from each group and give group members that grade.

9. **Test Reviewers.** Have students prepare each other for a test. They get bonus points if every group member scores above a preset level.

 10. **Composition Pairs.** Student A explains what s/he plans to write to Student B, while Student B takes notes or makes an outline. Together they plan the opening or thesis statement. Then Student B explains while Student A writes. They exchange outlines, and use them in writing their papers.

11. **Board Workers.** Students go together to the chalkboard. One can be the **Answer Suggester**, one the **Checker** to see if everyone agrees, and one the **Writer**.

12. **Problem Solvers.** Give groups a problem to solve. Each student must contribute to part of the solution. Groups can decide who does what, but they must show where all members contributed. Or, they can decide together, but each must be able to explain how to solve the problem.

13. **Computer Groups.** Students work together on the computer. They must agree on the input before it is typed in. One person is the **Keyboard Operator**, another the **Monitor Reader**, a third the **Verifier** (who collects opinions on the input from the other two and makes the final decision). Roles are rotated daily so everyone gets experience at all three jobs.

14. **Book Report Pairs.** Students interview each other on the books they read, then they report on their partner's book.

15. **Writing Response Groups.** Students read and respond to each other's papers three times:

    a. They mark what they like with a star and put a question mark anywhere there is something they don't understand or think is weak. Then they discuss the paper as a whole with the writer.

    b. They mark problems with grammar, usage, punctuation, spelling, or format and discuss it with the author.

c. They proofread the final draft and point out any errors for the author to correct.

Teachers can assign questions for students to answer about their group members' papers to help them focus on certain problems or skills.

16. **Skill Teachers/Concept Clarifiers.** Students work with each other on skills (like identifying adjectives in sentences or showing proof in algebra) and/or concepts (like "ecology" or "economics") until both can do or explain it easily.

17. **Group Reports.** Students research a topic together. Each one is responsible for checking at least one different source and writing at least three notecards of information. They write the report together; each person is responsible for seeing that h/her information is included. For oral reports, each must take a part and help each other rehearse until they are all at ease.

18. **Summary Pairs.** Have students alternate reading and orally summarizing paragraphs. One reads and summarizes while the other checks the paragraph for accuracy and adds anything left out. They alternate roles with each paragraph.

19. **Elaborating and Relating Pairs.** Have students elaborate on what they are reading and learning by relating it to what they already know about the subject. This can be done before and after reading a selection, listening to a lecture, or seeing a film.

20. **Playwrights.** Students write a play together, perhaps about a time period recently studied, practice, and perform it for the class.

A Few More Tips About Cooperative Start-Up

Some Ways to Ensure Positive Interdependence

1. One pencil, paper, or book given to a group
2. One paper written from a group
3. Task divided into jobs; it can't be finished unless all help
4. Pass one paper around the group, each member must do a part
5. Jigsaw materials; each person learns a part and then teaches it to the group
6. A reward (like bonus points) if everyone in the group succeeds

Some Ways to Ensure Individual Accountability

1. Students do the work first to bring to the group
2. Pick one student at random to orally answer questions studied by the group
3. Everyone writes, then certifies correctness of all papers; you pick one to grade
4. Listen and watch as students take turns orally rehearsing information
5. Assign jobs or roles to each student
6. Students get bonus points if all group members do well individually

Some Expected Behaviors to Tell Students

(Pick four or five that fit)

1. Everyone contributes and helps
2. Everyone listens to others with care
3. Encourage everyone in your group to participate
4. Praise helpful actions or good ideas
5. Ask for help if you need it
6. Check to make sure everyone understands
7. Stay with your group
8. Use quiet voices

Some Things To Do When Monitoring

1. Give immediate feedback and reinforcement for learning
2. Encourage oral elaboration and explanation
3. Reteach or add to teaching
4. Determine what group skills students have mastered
5. Encourage and praise use of good group skills
6. Determine what group skills to teach students next
7. Find out interesting things about your students

Some Ways to Process Group Interactions

Small Groups

1. What did your group do well in working together today?
2. What could your group do even better tomorrow?

Whole Class

1. What skills did we do well in working together today?
2. What skills could we do even better tomorrow?

Individual (Self)

1. What did you do well in helping your group today?
2. What could you do even better tomorrow?

Individual (Other)

1. Name one thing a group member did which helped your group.
2. Tell your group members that you appreciated their help.

Jigsawing Materials

One way to structure positive interdependence among group members is to use the jigsaw method of creating resource interdependence. The steps for structuring a "jigsaw" lesson are:

1. Distribute a set of materials to each group. The set needs to be divisible into the number of members of the group (2, 3, or 4 parts). Give each member one part of the set of materials.

2. Assign students the individualistic tasks of:

   a. Learning and becoming an expert on your material.

   b. Planning how to teach the material to the other members of the group.

3. Assign students the cooperative task of meeting with someone else in the class who is a member of another learning group and who has learned the same material and share ideas as to how the material may best be taught. This is known as an "expert pair" or "expert group."

4. Assign students the cooperative tasks of:

   a. Teaching their area of expertise to the other group members.

   b. Learning the material being taught by the other members.

5. Assess students' degree of mastery of all the material. Reward the groups whose members all reach the preset criteria of excellence.

Jigsaw is a flexible way of structuring positive interdependence among group members and teachers have developed many variations. Here are several modifications that are helpful in different circumstances:

1. Substitute pairs for individuals during Step 2.

2. Give students subtopics and have them use reference materials and the library to research their subtopic. This frees the teacher from having to arrange materials in advance.

3. Have the group write a report or give a class presentation on the overall topic, with the specification that it include all the subtopics presented in the group.

4. Prepare outlines or study guides of what each subtopic should cover and have students read the same text, organizing and becoming experts on the material highlighted by their outline or study guide.*

Some Favorite Roles

Roles are assigned to students in order to create positive interdependence and to teach students new skills. There are two types of roles to assign: **working roles** (like **Reader**, **Recorder**, and **Materials Handler**) and **skill roles** (like **Encourager**, **Checker**, and **Prober**). Both of these types help the group function and help students learn to be valuable group members. Students will learn new roles if those roles are carefully defined, watched for, and rewarded. The following are possible definitions of some roles to get you started.

----

* More specific instructions for each step of the jigsaw may be found in Cooperation in the Classroom by David W. Johnson and Roger T. Johnson. Edina, MN: Interaction Book Company, 1984.

Reader: Reads the group's material out loud to the group, carefully and with expression, so that group members can understand and remember it.

Writer: Carefully records the best answers of the group on the worksheet or paper, gets the group members to check and sign the paper, then turns it in to the teacher.

Materials Handler: Gets any materials or equipment needed by the group, keeps track of them, and puts them carefully away.

Encourager: Watches to make certain that everyone is participating, and invites reluctant or silent members to participate. Sample statements: *Jane, what do you think? Robert, do you have anything to add? Nancy, help us out. Juanita, what are your ideas on this?*

Checker: Checks on the comprehension or learning of group members by asking them to explain or summarize material learned or discussed. Sample statements: *Terry, why did we decide on this answer for number two? James, explain how we got this answer. Anne, summarize for us what we've decided here.*

Praiser: Helps members feel good about their contributions to the group by telling them how helpful they are. This is a good role to assign to help combat "put-downs." Sample statements: *That's a good idea, Al. Sharon, you're very helpful. Karen, I like the way you've helped us. Good job, John.*

Prober: In a pleasant way, keeps the group from superficial answers by not allowing the members to agree too quickly. Agrees when satisfied that the group has explored all the possibilities. Sample statements: *What other possibilities are there for this problem or questions? What else could we put here? Let's double-check this answer.*

Some other role possibilities include: **Noise Monitor** (uses a non-verbal signal to remind group members to quiet down), **Energizer** (energizes the group when it starts lagging), **Summarizer** (summarizes the material so that group members can check it again), **Asker for Help**, **Time Keeper**, **Question Asker**, and **Paraphraser**. Come up with roles that fit the task and your students.

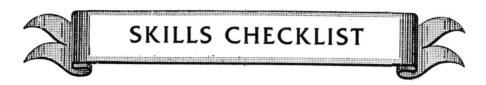

Check off the skills your students can do.
Star the skills you are currently teaching (no more than four!).
Put an arrow by the skill you will choose next
(when they are ready).

Forming Skills

_____ Moving into groups quietly

_____ Staying with the group

_____ Using quiet voices

_____ Encouraging everyone to participate

_____ Keeping hands and feet to self

_____ Looking at the group's paper

_____ Using people's names

_____ Looking at the speaker

_____ Using no "put-downs"

Functioning Skills

_____ Stating and restating the purpose of the assignment

_____ Setting or calling attention to time limits

_____ Offering procedures on how to most effectively do task

_____ Expressing support and acceptance verbally

_____ Expressing support and acceptance nonverbally

_____ Asking for help or clarification

_____ Offering to explain or clarify

_____ Paraphrasing and clarifying other members' contributions

_____ Energizing the group with humor, ideas, or enthusiasm

_____ Describing feelings when appropriate

Formulating Skills

_____ Summarizing the material aloud

_____ Seeking accuracy by correcting and/or adding to summaries

_____ Seeking elaboration by relating to other learning or knowledge

_____ Seeking clever ways of remembering ideas and facts

_____ Demanding vocalization of other members' reasoning processes

_____ Asking members to plan aloud how to teach material to others

Fermenting Skills

_____ Criticizing ideas without criticizing people

_____ Differentiating where there is disagreement

_____ Integrating different ideas into a single position

_____ Asking for justification of others' conclusions or ideas

_____ Extending other members' answers or conclusions

_____ Probing by asking questions that lead to deeper analysis

_____ Generating further answers

_____ Testing reality by checking group's work against instructions

Checklist for Teachers' Role in Cooperative Learning

Check off the areas you are comfortable doing.
Star the areas you are currently working to master.
Put an arrow by the area you will tackle next, when you are ready.

_____ Specifying academic objectives

_____ Specifying cooperative objectives

_____ Deciding on group size

_____ Assigning students to groups

_____ Arranging the room

_____ Planning materials

_____ Assigning roles

_____ Explaining the academic task

_____ Structuring positive interdependence

_____ Structuring individual accountability

_____ Structuring intergroup cooperation

_____ Explaining criteria for success

_____ Specifying desired behaviors

_____ Monitoring students' behavior

_____ Providing task assistance

_____ Intervening to teach collaborative skills

_____ Providing closure to the lesson

_____ Evaluating the quality and quantity of students' learning

_____ Having groups process their effectiveness

_____   Doing whole-class processing

_____   Having individuals process their effectiveness

_____   Teaching needed cooperative skills

_____   Observing for cooperative skills taught

_____   Giving feedback on cooperative skill use

_____   Rewarding skillful groups

_____   Rewarding skillful students

_____   Using student observers

_____   Demonstrating cooperative groups to other professionals

ADD-ON OBSERVATION SHEET

Start by teaching one skill and observing for it. Show students how well they do in practicing that skill; praise and otherwise reward their efforts. When they have mastered one skill, add and teach a second skill, etc.

DATE _____   PERIOD _____   OBSERVER _____

Cooperative Skills	Group Members			

Other Observation Notes:

···≫⊱⊰[COOPERATIVE LEARNING LESSON PLAN I   ]⊱⊰⊱···

TITLE _____

YOUR NAME _____

SCHOOL AND DISTRICT _____

SUBJECT AREA _____   GRADE LEVEL _____

LESSON SUMMARY _____

_____

_____

INSTRUCTIONAL OBJECTIVES _____

_____

_____

MATERIALS NEEDED _____

_____

_____

TIME REQUIRED _____   GROUP SIZE _____

ASSIGNMENT TO GROUPS _____

_____

ROLES   (Name and explain) _____

_____

_____

_____

_____

THE LESSON

TASK _____

_____

_____

_____

_____

_____

_____

_____

POSITIVE INTERDEPENDENCE _____

_____

_____

INDIVIDUAL ACCOUNTABILITY _____

_____

_____

CRITERIA FOR SUCCESS _____

_____

_____

EXPECTED BEHAVIORS _____

_____

_____

_____

MONITORING AND PROCESSING

MONITOR FOR _____

_____

_____

_____

INTERVENE IF _____

_____

_____

_____

PROCESS BY _____

_____

_____

_____

END BY _____

_____

_____

(Attach any materials needed to run the lesson)

COOPERATIVE LEARNING LESSON PLAN II

TITLE _____

TEACHER _____

SCHOOL AND DISTRICT _____

SUBJECT AREA _____ GRADE LEVEL _____

LESSON SUMMARY _____

_____

_____

INSTRUCTIONAL OBJECTIVES _____

_____

_____

MATERIALS NEEDED _____

_____

_____

TIME REQUIRED _____ GROUP SIZE _____

ASSIGNMENT TO GROUPS _____

_____

ROLES _____

_____

_____

THE LESSON

TASK _____

_____

_____

_____

_____

_____

_____

_____

Johnson, Johnson and Holubec

POSITIVE INTERDEPENDENCE _____

_____

_____

INDIVIDUAL ACCOUNTABILITY _____

_____

_____

CRITERIA FOR SUCCESS _____

_____

EXPECTED BEHAVIORS _____

_____

SOCIAL SKILL TEACHING

SKILL TAUGHT/PRACTICED _____

DEFINED _____

PHRASES _____

CRITERIA FOR SUCCESS _____

USE REWARDED BY _____

MONITORING AND PROCESSING

MONITORING BY: Teacher _____   Student _____   Both _____   Other _____

MONITOR FOR _____

_____

_____

INTERVENE IF _____

_____

_____

PROCESS BY _____

_____

_____

END BY _____

_____

(Attach materials and observation sheet)

Structuring Academic Controversies

For the past several years we have been training teachers and professors throughout North America in the use of structured academic controversies. The basic format for doing so consists of:

1. Choosing a topic that has content manageable by the students and on which at least two well-documented positions (pro and con) can be prepared. Topics on which we have developed curriculum units include: *Should the wolf be a protected species? Should coal be used as an energy source? Should nuclear energy be used as an energy source? Should the regulation of hazardous wastes be increased? Should the Boundary Waters Canoe Area be a national park? How should acid precipitation be controlled?* and many others.

2. Prepare the instructional materials so that group members know what position they have been assigned and where they can find supporting information.

3. Structure the controversy by:

   a. Assigning students to groups of four.

   b. Divide each group into two pairs. Assign pro and con positions to the pair.

   c. Highlight the cooperative goal of reaching a con-

sensus on the issue and writing a quality group report on which all members will be evaluated.

4. Conduct the controversy by (five class periods are recommended):

   a. Assign each pair the cooperative task of learning their position and its supporting arguments and information.

   b. Each pair presents their position to the other.

   c. The group discusses the issue, critically evaluating the opposing position and its rationale, defending their position, and comparing the strengths and weaknesses of the two positions.

   d. The pairs reverse perspectives and positions by presenting the opposing position as sincerely and forcefully as they can.

   e. The group drops their advocacy, reaches a decision, and writes a group report that includes their joint position and the supporting evidence and rationale. A test on the content covered in both positions may be given with the groups whose members all score above the preset criteria of excellence receiving bonus points.

A more detailed description of conducting academic controversies may be found in Johnson, Johnson and Smith (1986) and Johnson and Johnson (1987). Peggy Tiffany, a 4th-grade teacher in Wilmington, Vermont, regularly conducts an academic controversy on whether or not the wolf should be a protected species. She gives students the cooperative assignment of writing a report on the wolf in which they summarize what they have learned about the wolf and recommend the procedures they think are best for regulating wolf populations and preserving wolves within the continental United States.   Students are randomly assigned to groups of four, ensuring that

both male and female and high-, medium-, and low-achieving students are all in the same group.   The group is divided into two pairs and one pair is assigned the position of an environmental organization that believes wolves should be a protected species and the other pair is assigned the position of farmers and

ranchers who believe that wolves should not be a protected species.   Each side is given a packet of articles, stories, and information that sup- ports their position.   During the first class period each pair develops their position and plans how to present the best case possible to the other pair.   Near the end of the period pairs are encouraged to compare notes with pairs from other groups who represent the same position. During the second class period each pair makes their presentation.   Each member of the pair has to participate in the presentation.   The opposing pair are encouraged to take notes and listen carefully.   During the third class period the group discusses the issue following a set of rules to help them criticize ideas without criticizing people, differentiate the two positions, and assess the degree of evidence and logic supporting each position.   During the first half of the fourth hour the pairs reverse perspectives and present each other's positions.

Grey Wolf

Students drop their advocacy positions, clarify their understanding of each other's information and rationale and begin work on their group report. The first half of the fifth period is spent finalizing their report. The report is evaluated on the basis of the quality of the writing, the evaluation of opinion and evidence, and the oral presentation of the report to the class. The students then each take an individual test on the wolf and, if every member of the group achieves up to criteria, they all receive the bonus points. Finally, during the sixth class period each group makes a 10-minute presentation to the entire class summarizing their report. All four members of the group are required to participate orally in the presentation. Within this lesson positive interdependence is structured by having each group arrive at a consensus and submit one written report and making one presentation, by jigsawing the materials to the pairs within the group, and by giving bonus points to members if all members learn the basic information contained in the two positions and score well on the test. Individual accountability is structured by having each member of the pair orally participate in the presentation of the position and in the perspective reversal, each member of the group orally participates in the group presentation, and each member takes an individual test on the material. The collaborative skills emphasized are those involved in systematically advocating an intellectual position and evaluating and criticizing the position advocated by others, as well as the skills involved in synthesis and consensual decision making. Numerous academic and social benefits are derived from participating in such structured controversies (Johnson & Johnson, 1987; Johnson, Johnson, & Smith, 1986).

REFERENCES

Johnson, D. W., & Johnson, R. T. (1984).   Cooperation in the classroom.
Edina, MN: Interaction Book Company.

Johnson, D. W., & Johnson, R. T. (1987).   Learning together and alone:
Cooperative, competitive, and individualistic learning (2nd ed.).
Englewood Cliffs, NJ: Prentice-Hall.

Johnson, D. W., Johnson, R. T., & Smith, K. A. (1986).   Academic conflict
among students: Controversy and learning.   In R. Feldman (Ed.),
The social psychology of education.   Cambridge: Cambridge University
Press.

Johnson, R. T., & Johnson, D. W. (1985).   Cooperative learning: Warm-ups,
grouping strategies and group activities.   Edina, MN: Interaction
Book Company.

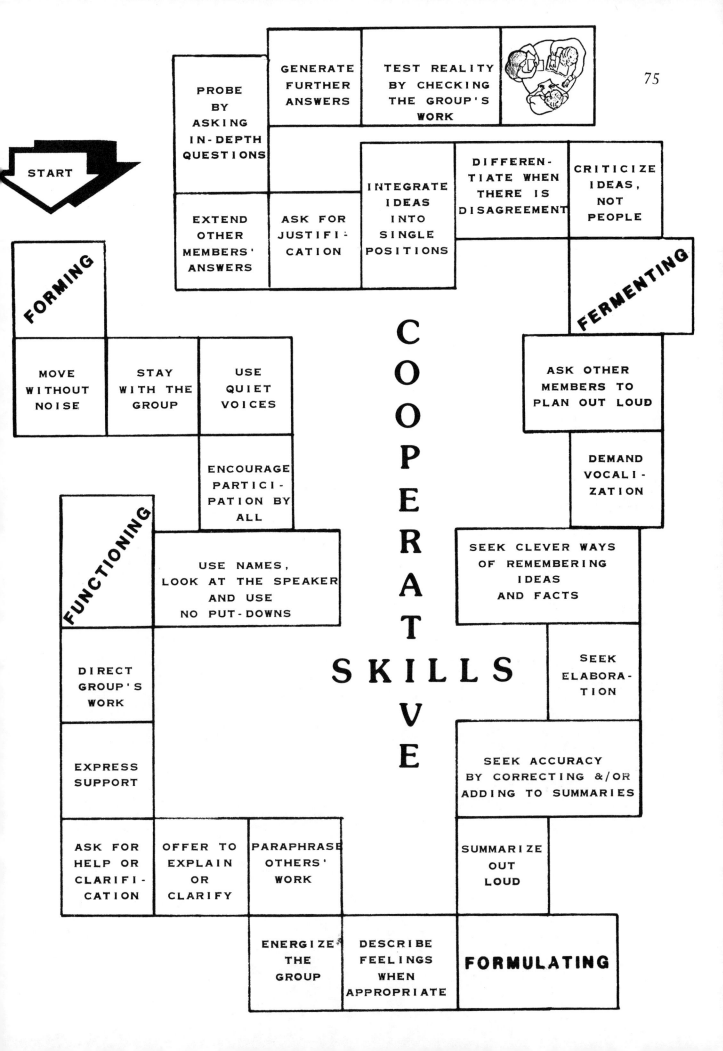

START

PROBE BY ASKING IN-DEPTH QUESTIONS

GENERATE FURTHER ANSWERS

TEST REALITY BY CHECKING THE GROUP'S WORK

EXTEND OTHER MEMBERS' ANSWERS

ASK FOR JUSTIFI-CATION

INTEGRATE IDEAS INTO SINGLE POSITIONS

DIFFEREN-TIATE WHEN THERE IS DISAGREEMENT

CRITICIZE IDEAS, NOT PEOPLE

FORMING

FERMENTING

MOVE WITHOUT NOISE

STAY WITH THE GROUP

USE QUIET VOICES

ASK OTHER MEMBERS TO PLAN OUT LOUD

ENCOURAGE PARTICI-PATION BY ALL

DEMAND VOCALI-ZATION

FUNCTIONING

USE NAMES, LOOK AT THE SPEAKER AND USE NO PUT-DOWNS

SEEK CLEVER WAYS OF REMEMBERING IDEAS AND FACTS

C O O P E R A T I V E

DIRECT GROUP'S WORK

SEEK ELABORA-TION

S K I L L S

EXPRESS SUPPORT

SEEK ACCURACY BY CORRECTING &/OR ADDING TO SUMMARIES

ASK FOR HELP OR CLARIFI-CATION

OFFER TO EXPLAIN OR CLARIFY

PARAPHRASE OTHERS' WORK

SUMMARIZE OUT LOUD

ENERGIZE THE GROUP

DESCRIBE FEELINGS WHEN APPROPRIATE

FORMULATING

Primary

Making a Long Train

ROGER and DAVID JOHNSON

Minneapolis,
MN

Subject Area: Problem Solving

Grade Level: Preschool/Kindergarten

Lesson Summary: Students in groups of three build a long train using three different colors of blocks.

Instructional Objectives: Students will realize that to build a long train they will have to work together and create one train using all three colors of blocks.

Materials:

ITEM	NUMBER NEEDED
Red blocks (8)	One set per group
Blue blocks (8)	One set per group
Green blocks (8)	One set per group
Red hat or badge*	One per group
Blue hat or badge*	One per group
Green hat or badge*	One per group
(Crayons -- optional)	One box per group

*Can be made from construction paper

Time Required: Thirty minutes

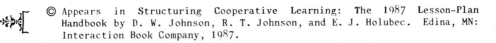

≈ Decisions ≈

Group Size: Three

Assignment
To Groups: Teacher assigned to be heterogeneous (gender, ethnic back-
                 ground, etc.)

Roles: Each student is an **Engineer** for their color of blocks.

≈ The Lesson ≈

Instructional Task:

The task is to build a long train with each car (block) touching
another car (block). It is best not to get too specific on the task
beyond this basic statement as the students need to decide on how to
do this. It is interesting to note
whether they want to build three
different trains initially or will
immediately go to a single train.

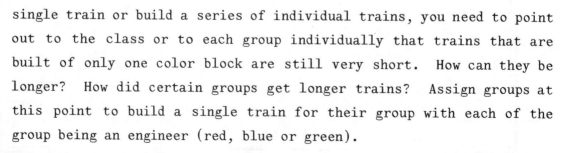

Positive Interdependence:

After giving students a moment to
see if they immediately go to a
single train or build a series of individual trains, you need to point
out to the class or to each group individually that trains that are
built of only one color block are still very short. How can they be
longer? How did certain groups get longer trains? Assign groups at
this point to build a single train for their group with each of the
group being an engineer (red, blue or green).

Individual Accountability:

Explain in the directions that only the engineer with the red hat (or badge) can move the red cars, only the engineer with the green hat can move the green cars and only the engineer with the blue hat can move the blue cars. Since some of the students may not know their colors, the hats (or badges) are important. They each have a job to do as the red engineer is responsible for getting the red cars into the train and no other engineer can touch those cars (blocks).

Criteria for Success:

Any group which can get a train longer than the teacher's stick (chosen to be longer than 16 blocks, but shorter than 24) is successful. The criteria should be introduced after the positive interdependence and individual accountability are clear.

Expected Behaviors:

These can be volunteered by the young engineers themselves after their initial start and when they realize that they are to build only one train for their group.   Make sure that they include: – Listening to each other's ideas with care (i.e., look at the person who is speaking and don't talk when someone else is talking).

   – Remembering the rules of only touching the blocks that match your hat (badge).

   – Giving each other ideas and advice on how to build the long train.

≈ Monitoring and Processing ↝

Monitoring: This is a fascinating lesson to observe as you will often see students wanting to build their own (short) train without involving the others. When they realize that they need to work together to build a long train, you can get many

different patterns from all red, then blue, then green
(which tells you something about the group) to a random pattern.   Look for an organizer in the group
when you see a red, blue, green --
red, blue, green alternating pat-
tern.   Note the patterns for each
group of students or have them do
it themselves for you by drawing
their train when they are finished (only
the red hat can use the red crayon, blue hat blue crayon,
green hat green crayon).   Include in the data keeping for
each group the comments made as they work which indicate
why they are using that pattern and positive examples of
the required behaviors.

Intervening: You may need to spend some time with a group where students
still do not work together to make a long train (longer
than your stick).   Sometimes it has to be made doubly clear
to some students that they cannot be successful alone with
only their color on this task and have to work as a group.
In fact two students working together can not build a long
enough train.   They need all three group members to be successful.   Don't intervene too quickly, but instead watch
some of the arguments develop and see if the group can
resolve them.   You should enforce the rule about the
engineer with the right color touching the matching blocks.

Ending: Lead the students on a trip to see all the trains.   Ask
them why they are not all the same.   What can you tell
about this group by how the blocks are placed?

Processing: Pull the class up around you.   If you have pictures, you
can ask individual groups to report on their pattern and
why it developed that way.   Ask them to raise their hands

if they actively listened (are they doing it now?). Have them say so if they have an especially good listener in their group. Check out the other specified behaviors if there is time. Comment yourself about the things you saw happening in the groups with the specific examples of positive group behavior. Be sure and direct your compliments most of the time to the group and the class rather than individuals to avoid competition.

AUTHOR'S NOTE

I recently read a newspaper editorial which started: **Everything I've needed in Life, I learned in Kindergarten.** Although this may be stretching it some, a lot of good things are started early in school when the major concern is how to get twenty-some individuals living peacefully in the same room together for one hundred and seventy-six days. The earlier we start on executive training, the better. As some push for more academics in Kindergarten and strive to make it look more like the older grades, keep in mind that one of the basic reasons for school is to send students into communities, careers, marriages and families skillful in interacting with other people and maintaining those links over time. We should probably be trying to make the rest of school look more like Kindergarten. For the most part we start school off right, but quickly get sidetracked into classrooms where students sit in rows, are not allowed to talk, and students are isolated from one another. It's a sad commentary on school-life after Kindergarten to hear that anyone "learned it all" at that level.

Bead Sequencing

BRITT VASQUEZ

Sacramento, CA

Subject Area: Reading Readiness

Grade Level: Preschool

Lesson Summary: In pairs the students will cooperate to duplicate a given sequence of beads.

Instructional Objectives: Students will gain practice in listening to directions.

Materials:

ITEM	NUMBER NEEDED
Shoe-string	One per group
Set of colored stringing beads	One per group
Set of pattern cards	One per group
Listening hat*	One per student

*Prior to this lesson, the students can build Listening Hats from construction paper (similar to Mouseketeer Ears).

Time Required: Fifteen minutes.

≋ Decisions ≋

Group Size: Two

**Assignment
To Groups:**   Teacher assigned, with one more-skilled and one less-skilled member in each group.

≋ The Lesson ≋

Instructional Task:

Today you and your partner will string beads. You will string the beads in a certain way. I will tell you that way.

You will work together, in pairs, with one of you stringing, and the other talking to make your beads look exactly like the picture I will give you. You will also be practicing good listening. Each of you will wear your listening hats to help you remember to use good listening. Who can tell me some things we do and see when we are doing good listening?

One of you will be the Teller. One of you will be the Stringer. To make your beads look exactly like the picture, lay the picture on your table with the star at the top. Look at the side of your picture that has the smiley face on it. That is where you will start. Look at

the first bead in the picture. Look at its color. That is the color bead you, the Teller, will pick out of the box and give to the Stringer to put on the shoe-string.

If the Stringer agrees that it is the right bead, the Stringer puts that one on. If the Stringer doesn't think that is the right bead, he or she should say:

"I think the right bead is the _____ because _____"

and say why you think a different bead is right. When you both decide on the right bead, when you both agree, the Stringer puts it on.

Look at the next bead. Look at the color. That is the next color bead the Teller takes out of the box and gives the Stringer to put on the string. Go on to the next and the next until you have all beads in the picture on your shoe-string.

(Check for understanding) *Who can tell me what we are going to do?*

Positive Interdependence:

Remember that your group is going to agree on each bead so that when you're done, yours will look just like the picture.

Criteria for Success:

I will know you did a good job if:
- *Only the Teller picks up the bead from the box.*
- *Only the Stringer strings the bead.*
- *All the beads on your string are like the beads in the picture.*
- *Both of you listen very carefully to each other.*

Expected Behaviors:

The Teller needs to talk very nicely and very clearly. The Stringer needs to listen very carefully so that she or he gets just the right bead on the string, in the right order. Both the Stringer and the Teller must agree that the beads on the string are the same as the beads in the picture.

What kind of voices will I hear if the Teller is talking very nicely? What will I see if the Stringer is carefully listening and stringing?

∼ Monitoring and Processing ∼

Monitoring: The teacher will observe.

I will watch each pair of workers. I will watch for Teller using a soft voice, the Stringer looking at the Teller and not talking, and only the Stringer touching the beads. I will look to see that all the beads are just like the picture.

Processing: The teacher will call on various individuals to respond to each of the following:

- Do you think the **Teller** did a good job in your group?
- Do you think the **Stringer** did a good job in your group?
- Do the beads your group strung look like the picture?

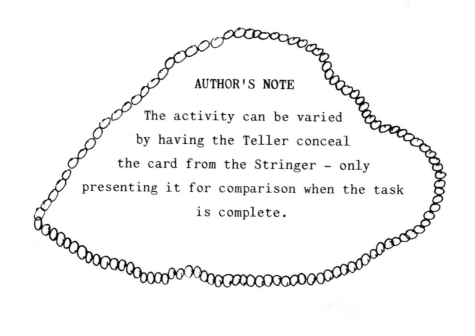

AUTHOR'S NOTE

The activity can be varied
by having the Teller conceal
the card from the Stringer – only
presenting it for comparison when the task
is complete.

Creative Thinking

NANCY WHITSON

Snohomish,
WA

Subject Area: Language Arts

Grade Level: Primary

Lesson Summary: After hearing the story of **Nimby** by Jasper Tomkins, students create a picture of something else Nimby and the island could have been together.

Instructional
  Objectives: Students will gain practice in creative thinking by coming up with and drawing together a new idea based on the story.

Materials:

ITEM	NUMBER NEEDED
Nimby by Jasper Tomkins	One for teacher
Drawing paper	One per group
Crayons	One set per group

Time Required: Thirty minutes

≈ Decisions ≈

Group Size: Three

Assignment
To Groups: Random, by counting off

Roles: None

≈ The Lesson ≈

Instructional Task:

I read the class the story of **Nimby** by Jasper Tomkins. Nimby is a playful young cloud who always wanted to make something with his cloud body instead of just being an ordinary cloud like all the other clouds. The older clouds didn't approve of his playful antics and he finally floats away from the other clouds and makes all kinds of different things with his body. Nobody pays any attention to him, and he becomes very lonely and wants a friend. One day, while he was  floating over the ocean, he discovers a small island who also likes to make different things with his shape. They become friends; together, they make many different things.

Following the story, the group assignment is to think about and create a picture of something else that Nimby and the island could have made together. In order to be successful, the group members have to share their ideas with each other, come to an agreement on what to make, and then each contribute to the drawing. Each then takes a part in showing and explaining their picture to the class.

Positive Interdependence:

Tell students that you want one picture from the group that they all agree upon and can explain. They will have only one piece of paper to draw on and one box of crayons for the group. They must all agree on what the group is going to draw and who in the group is going to draw what before anyone can start drawing.

Individual Accountability:

Tell the students that each of them must share their ideas and contribute to the drawing. When they explain their picture to the class, one of them will hold the picture, one of them will explain what part of the picture Nimby is, and the other will explain what part the island is.

Criteria for Success:

If they agree upon and draw one picture together that shows a new thing Nimby and the island could have been, they have been successful.

Expected Behaviors:

Tell them you expect to see them working together, agreeing upon what they are going to draw before they start, and making sure that everyone in the group has a part to draw (sharing).

∽ Monitoring and Processing ∾

Monitoring: During the group work, listen for ways in which they are coming to agreement and sharing with each other.

Intervening: Stop the groups and help them if they are having difficulty in agreeing or sharing. Also, reinforce groups who come to agreement and who share in the drawing of the picture.

Ending: Have the students share their pictures with the class, with one member holding the picture, another explaining what part of the picture Nimby is, and the other explaining what part the island is.

Processing: After they have told about their pictures, ask the students to think about ways in which their group shared ideas, resources, and responsibilities during the activity. Then have them thank their group members for helping and pat themselves on the back for a job well done!

AUTHOR'S NOTE

The students came up with some really different and unique ideas as they worked together in their groups. One of the pictures showed Nimby as the body of a cat and the island as the tail, complete with trees growing on it. In another, the island was a turtle shell and Nimby was the head, feet, and tail going in and out. In others, the island was a volcano and Nimby was the lava erupting from it; the island was a chalkboard and Nimby was the chalk; the island was a fishing boat and Nimby was the motor; Nimby was the white part of a penguin and the island was the black part; and the island was a steam ship and Nimby was the smoke coming out of the smokestack.

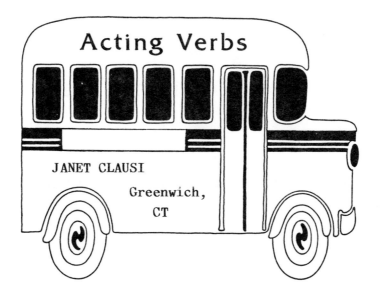

Acting Verbs

JANET CLAUSI

Greenwich, CT

Subject Area: Language Arts

Grade Level: Primary

Lesson Summary: Students learn about verbs as action words by acting them out for the class to guess, first individually, then in pairs.

Instructional Objectives: Students will experience and identify verbs as action words.

Materials:

ITEM	NUMBER NEEDED
Set of pictures of people demonstrating verbs*; each picture shows one verb	More cards than children in classroom

*Verb Concept Cards, F4320P, DLM Teaching Resources, P.O. Box 4000, Allen, Texas 75002 is a source.

Time Required: Forty-five minutes to an hour

≈ Decisions ≈

Group Size: Two

Assignment to Groups: Random. The students are assigned to groups of two by counting off around the circle. Each group is assigned a place to work as the groups are formed.

Classroom Arrangement: To start, the desks are pushed to the sides of the room and the students and teacher sit in a large circle in the middle of the room, either on the floor or on chairs; there is a large performing space in the center. When the groups of two are working, they use spaces around the room that are reasonably separated from each other.

Roles: None

≈ The Lesson ≈

Instructional Task:

Part 1: Have the class answer the question: *What is a verb?* with enough discussion so that it is clear to everyone. Then explain that you have a pile of cards with pictures of verbs on them and each child will have a chance to choose a card and act out the verb pictured on the card for the children to identify. (I like to have the cards mounted on a dif- ferent colored cardboard and then laminated to that the child has a choice to make even before she sees a picture.) Have each child act out his chosen verb before the large group. Be sure and look at the card that has been chosen so that you can help the actor with the action or help the audience guess the verb. (Some- times more than one verb can be suggested by the same picture, i.e., a picture of a boxer could be identified as **boxing, fighting, punch- ing,** etc.) Tell the audience that they are a large cooperative group

for the actor, watching and listening carefully in order to arrive at the answer.   Tell them to wait until the actor has finished before raising hands to guess.   Have the actor choose the child to guess the verb.

Part 2:   When each child has had a turn, have the class count off to form groups of two.   Explain that each pair is to decide on an action word, a verb, that they will both act out for the rest of the class. They must also decide how they are going to act out the verb and which one of them will choose the children to guess their work. Tell them that when they have made their decisions, they are to return to the circle and sit next to their partner.   Then assign each pair a place to work.   When all of the pairs are ready, the acting and guessing proceeds as in **Part 1**.

Positive Interdependence:

Both of you must take part in acting out the verb you have chosen, and you both must agree on your decisions.

Individual Accountability:

You are to help your partner make the decisions and act out the verb.

Criteria for Success:

You will be successful if the audience can correctly identify your verb.

Expected Behaviors:

*We are working on our **forming skills**.   Remember to move quickly and quietly to your assigned work spaces, keep your voices quiet so you don't disturb other groups, and stay in your space until you are ready to join the circle.*

∽ Monitoring and Processing ∼

Monitoring: Observe to be sure that all the children are participating in their group. Since this is such an active lesson, the child who is watching another group while her partner is working is easy to spot. It is also easy to hear the groups that are working too loudly.

Intervening: Because there has been a large group practice, there is seldom any need to do more than remind a group of the skills that are being practiced.

Processing: After the lesson, ask the children to discuss their behaviors during the lesson. How did they think they moved into their groups? Did they keep quiet voices? Did they stay in their groups? Add your observations to the discussion.

fly

   flew

blow

   blew

   slide

     slid

buck

   bucked

ake

baked

catch

   caught

   smell

     smelled

build

   built

arry

  carried

stretch

   stretched

paint

painted

fish

fished

roar

roared

study

studi

dance

danced

dive

dived

play

played

cook

cooked

swing

swung

crow

crowed

le

smiled

chop

chopped

listen

listened

point

pointed

pull

pulled

skate

skated

ave

saved

carve

carved

talk

talked

row

rowed

Reading Buddies

MARY R. CARNICELLI
Auburn,
NY

Subject Area: Reading

Grade Level: Elementary

Lesson Summary: Students read a story from their readers in pairs, alternating paragraphs.

Instructional Objectives: Students will gain practice in the oral reading skills of fluency and expression, with the added benefit of increased comprehension.

Materials:

ITEM	NUMBER NEEDED
Reading text	One per student

Time Required: Thirty minutes (depending on length of story)

≈ Decisions ≈

Group Size: Two

**Assignment
to Groups:**   Teacher assigned, with a fluent reader teamed with a less
fluent reader.

Roles: **Reader** and **Listener**; they will alternate roles with each
paragraph.

≈ The Lesson ≈

Instructional Task:

 *You are to take turns and each read a paragraph while
the other listens. Offer help to decode and blend
if help is requested by your partner.*

Positive Interdependence:

*You will read one story together, alternating reading with each para-
graph.*

Individual Accountability:

*Read your paragraphs the best you can, asking your partner for help
if you need it. Listen carefully to your partner's paragraphs and
give him or her help if needed.*

Criteria for Success:

*Groups which help each other read with expression and fluency will be
chosen to dramatize the story to the class (or a lower grade).*

Expected Behaviors

*I expect to see you keeping your place in the book, listening care-
fully to your partner, reading clearly and with expression while*

paying attention to punctuation marks, and helping your partner if needed. I want you to continue to read until I tell you to stop, be patient with your partner, and offer to help.

≋ Monitoring and Processing ≋

Monitoring: Circulate, listening for fluency and expression and watching to make certain they are doing the expected behaviors.

Intervening: Intervene if groups need help with the reading or expected behaviors.

Processing: As a whole class, ask the students whether they listened carefully and helped their partners. Tell them what you saw them do well and you saw that would help them do better next time.

Closing: Stress the importance of fluency and expression in relation to comprehension.

AUTHOR'S NOTE

This lesson could be expanded to
(1) groups of three students; (2) one text to be passed
around the group, thus forcing better listening
skills and positive interdependence; or
(3) a list of comprehension questions for the group
to complete collaboratively.

Space Pioneers

JEAN CROCKETT

Vancouver,
BC

105

Subject Area: Social Studies

Grade Level: Primary

Lesson Summary: Students will group to form a family prior to moving to a new community in space.

Instructional Objectives: Students will determine the survival skills, cooperative efforts, and materials needed to build a space community.

Materials:

ITEM	NUMBER NEEDED
Gym mat (or a suitable arrangement of of four chairs)	One per group
Pencil	One per greoup
Space Community Worksheet	One per group

Time Required: One class period

≈ Decisions ≈

Group Size: Four

Assignment
To Groups: Teacher assigned with sex and ability-level heterogeneity.

Roles: Recorder: Student who assumes oldest familial role in the
                 space group will record the family name and list of space
                 needs.

≈ The Lesson ≈

Instructional Task:

Students choose a position/role within the new space family. Make the
stipulation that each family may include only one father, one mother,

and no one can be younger than in real life.
Suggest additional roles of grandparents, teenagers, aunts, uncles.

Then the family selects a group surname. It may
by the "father's" name or one preferred
generally by the group.

Finally, the family generates a list of 15 items it considers most
important in building a new community. (Remind them that space suits
are an essential first item.)

Positive Interdependence:

The group members must come to consensus on the list of survival
items and sign the sheet with their actual first names and the chosen
family surname.

Individual Accountability:

Any member of the family can be called on to read the selected items and explain the importance of any given item.

Criteria for Success:

The family agrees on a name and list and behaves in a way that would make it an important part of the new community.

Expected Behaviors:

Tell the students that you will be watching for the following forming skills:

1. Moving without noise
2. Staying with the group
3. Using 30 centimeter voices
4. Using names
5. Looking at the speaker
6. Helping complete the group's work

In addition, you will be listening for clarifying questions.

≈ Monitoring and Processing ≈

Monitoring: Teacher will use the observation sheet to record the frequency of use of the forming skills. Any clarifying questions may be noted verbatim on the sheet for later sharing.

Processing: Call on family members randomly to discuss how they worked together as a family in the new community. Ask what they might do to improve. Share with the class any clarifying questions you heard.

Ending: Choose a member from each group to contribute one item from his/her family's list. Put this "super-list" on the blackboard. When this discussion is complete, assemble the mats (or chairs) and families into a lift-off position. Using space music and guiding their imagery, the rocket blasts off, leaves Earth, flies past clouds, planets, moons, galaxies and stars before landing on the new planet. The students don their spacesuits and step onto their new community!

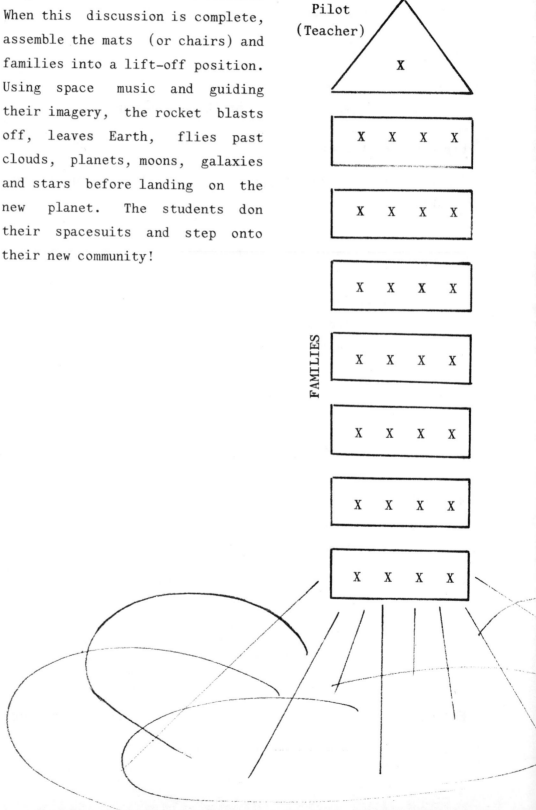

SPACE PLAN

These are the things we need when
we start our space community.

_____   _____

_____   _____

_____   _____

_____   _____

_____   _____

_____   _____

Signed:

_____   _____

_____   _____

Composing Riddles

KAREN SCHROEDER

Lincoln,
NE

Subject Area: Language Arts

Grade Level: Primary

Lesson Summary: After being given a pattern as a model, students try composing riddles together.

**Instructional
  Objectives:** Students will understand the skill in making a riddle pattern and gain practice in answering riddles.

Materials:

ITEM	NUMBER NEEDED
Pencils	One per group
Paper	Several sheets per group
Crayons	One set per group

Time Required: Thirty minutes

≈ Decisions ≈

Group Size: Three

**Assignment
To Groups:**   Random, by having the students count off, or teacher assigned with a good writer in each group.

Roles: **Riddle Writer:** Writes the riddle for the group

Riddle Reader: Reads the riddle while it is being written and later reads it to the class

Riddle Checker: Checks to see that the riddle fits the pattern and makes certain everyone likes each line of the riddle

≈ The Lesson ≈

Instructional Task:

Write the following riddle pattern on the chalkboard:

Who am I?

I have four feet.

I like bones.

I say bow-wow.

Who am I?

Tell the children this is called a riddle. Explain that a riddle does not tell who or what it is about. Instead it gives clues. We use the clues to figure out who or what the riddle is about. Have the children answer the riddle. Explain that each group is to write one riddle using the pattern on the board, and then will illustrate their riddle. When everyone is finished, they will show their riddle to the class for everyone to guess. Each group's riddle will be formed into a riddle booklet.

?

Positive Interdependence:

The group is to write one riddle and everyone must do his or her job in order to be successful.

Individual Accountability:

Each member will have a job in the group (explain and assign the roles).

Criteria for Success:

The group is successful when it has finished the task.

Expected Behaviors:

I expect you to stay with your group, help your partner, and ask your partner for help when you need it.

≈ Monitoring and Processing ≈

Monitoring: While the groups work, observe for your students under-standing how to use a pattern to create a riddle. Look also for good use of cooperative skills.

Intervening: Give help where you think it is needed.

Ending: Bring the class back together and have each group share its riddle pattern. Ask if all the riddles followed the desig-nated pattern.

Processing: Have the students tell what people did which helped their group work together. Add your own observations. Then, ask them what would help the groups work even better next time.

Reprinted from Structuring Cooperative Learning: The 1980 Handbook edited by Virginia M. Lyons. Edina, MN: Interaction Book Company.

Teacher Observation Sheet

	Monday	Tuesday	Wednes	Thurs	Friday
Listens to each other					
Asks if doesn't know					
Encourages each other					
Says kind things					

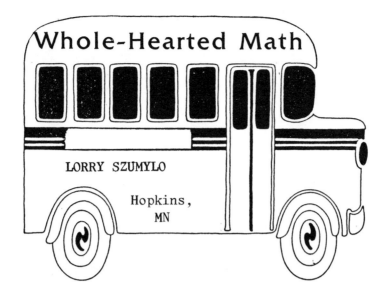

Whole-Hearted Math

LORRY SZUMYLO

Hopkins, MN

Subject Area: Math

Grade Level: Second grade (enrichment)

Lesson Summary: Comparing fractions with like numerators or denominators

Instructional Objectives:

1. To teach what part of a set of distinct objects has a given characteristic

2. To teach methods of comparing and ordering fractions with like numerators or like denominators utilizing the greater than/less than (> <) signs

3. To select a fraction and be able to tell what part is shaded

Materials:

ITEM	NUMBER NEEDED
Computer*	One (or?)
MECC Growgins' Fractions Disk	One
Candy Hearts (20 per color)	One set per group
Small paper cups (1 per color)	One set per group
Fraction Skill Sheet	One per group
Group Processing Sheet	One per group

*Note: If more than one computer is available, assign as many groups as can be accomodated--on a rotational basis.

Time Required: 40 minutes

≈ Decisions ≈

Group Size: Four

Assignment
To Groups: Teacher assigned allowing for heterogeneity in sex and
                   ability

Roles: **Guide:** Calls on group members for participation by all
                   members in the group. Clarifies directions if neces-
                   sary.

                   Checker: Makes sure every group member agrees with the
                   answer. Keeps group on task.

                   Writer: Is responsible for materials. Reports results.
                   Checks for names on skill sheets. Types at the computer.

                   Encourager: Listens   for   support   and   acceptance.
                   Encourages positive statements.

≈ The Lesson ≈

✳ Instructional Task:

   Begin this fraction lesson for young children with a whole-class
   presentation of the goals. Then group the students. If possible,
   have at least one group working at the computer with the other groups
   performing the same task on their worksheets. There is value in
   having the students alternate between working the problems on the computer and on the worksheet, so a rotation system would be the ideal
   option.

Tell the students they will be deciding on the fraction of each color of hearts in paper cups and will complete the skill sheet while working cooperatively. Groups will work on each item together and agree on what will be written on the paper or typed on the computer.

Positive Interdependence:

Sharing the goal that the group wishes to accomplish by asking questions, agreeing, and understanding.

Individual Accountability:

1. Students will be able to compare like numerators and denominators and place them in the correct order by size. They will be called on randomly to solve problems.
2. Students will be able to relate fraction of each color of candy hearts in cups.

Criteria for Success:

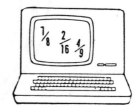

90% of work completed correctly
100% of candy heart assignment

Expected Behaviors:

Everyone participating with good listening skills. Remaining a responsible member of the group.

≋ Monitoring and Processing ≋

Monitoring: Teacher walks around the room observing and tallying group interaction.

Intervening: The teacher intervenes to solve problems and teach skills only when necessary. Problems should be turned back to the group to solve. Teacher acts as a consultant.

Processing: Teacher: Shares collected data with students.
                Students: Complete the Group Processing Sheet.

Closure: 1. Applause and praise for completed tasks
                2. Discussion of skills (social) to improve for next time

NOTE:

M & Ms or Peanuts
may be
substituted for
candy
hearts.

Johnson, Johnson and Holubec

Names
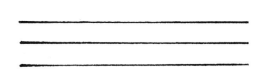

SKILLSHEET: FRACTIONS

1.   Shade in 2/3 of each set.

   a.    b.   c.

2.   Fill in < or > in each box.

   a. $\dfrac{2}{3} \square \dfrac{6}{3}$ b. $\dfrac{4}{6} \square \dfrac{2}{6}$ c. $\dfrac{1}{2} \square \dfrac{2}{2}$

   d. $\dfrac{3}{4} \square \dfrac{1}{4}$ e. $\dfrac{5}{5} \square \dfrac{7}{5}$ f. $\dfrac{16}{8} \square \dfrac{30}{8}$

   g. $\dfrac{2}{3} \square \dfrac{2}{6}$ h. $\dfrac{4}{8} \square \dfrac{4}{9}$ i. $\dfrac{5}{8} \square \dfrac{5}{6}$

   j. $\dfrac{4}{9} \square \dfrac{2}{9}$ k. $\dfrac{9}{13} \square \dfrac{11}{13}$ l. $\dfrac{10}{13} \square \dfrac{10}{17}$

3.   Place the following fractions in order from smallest to largest.

   a. $\dfrac{2}{3}$, $\dfrac{6}{3}$, $\dfrac{1}{3}$ _____

   b. $\dfrac{2}{5}$, $\dfrac{9}{5}$, $\dfrac{4}{5}$ _____

   c. $\dfrac{2}{13}$, $\dfrac{2}{16}$, $\dfrac{2}{15}$ _____

   d. $\dfrac{7}{8}$, $\dfrac{7}{20}$, $\dfrac{7}{16}$ _____

GROUP PROCESSING

Did everyone contribute ideas?

Did we share our materials?

Did we ask for everyone's ideas?

Did we make sure everyone in the group understood?

Did we help, encourage, and finish our work?

Spelling

DIANE BROWNE

Hopkins, MN

Subject Area: Spelling

Grade Level: Primary

Lesson Summary: Students learn spelling words together.

**Instructional
  Objectives:**   Students will learn to read and write spelling words and know their definitions.

Materials:

ITEM	NUMBER NEEDED
Sesame Street character role tags	One set per group
Spelling worksheets	One per student
Pencils	One per student
Teacher Observation Sheet*	One for teacher

* **Note:** The Teacher Observation Sheet from an earlier lesson (see page 114) would also be appropriate for this lesson.

Time Required: One spelling session

≈ Decisions ≈

Group Size: Three

**Assignment
To Groups:**   Teacher assigned, with one high, one low, and one middle achieving student in each group.

Roles: The Count = The Teller

Ernie = The Asker

The Cookie Monster = The Listener

≈ The Lesson ≈

Instructional Task:

Today, instead of having you do your work all alone, I'm going to let you work together and be teachers for each other (hand out the role tags to tape on each student). *Before we begin, each one of you is going to have a little job. Those of you who are The Count today are going to tell the people in your group what your task is and when it's their turn. Ernie is going to make sure everyone understands or asks when they don't get it. And The Cookie Monster is going to make sure we all listen to each other. I am going to listen in while you work and see how the Sesame Street characters are doing with their roles and give a quick report when the work is done. Also, The Count in each group will report on how well his or her group worked together. All of you will turn in your papers, but The Count will put his or her paper on top of the group's papers, and that paper will be the one graded to see if the group earns a star. Be sure that all the papers look the same as The Count's paper and that everyone knows how to read, spell, and tell the meaning of the words.*

Explain how to do the spelling worksheet you chose to use with this lesson. Then add: *Your group must agree on each answer before you can write it on your own paper. Then, make sure that each of you writes the word four times on your own worksheet. When you are finished, check everyone's paper to make sure all answers are correct. After that, stack your papers together and put The Count's paper on top. Sign The Count's paper to show you agree with those answers.*

Positive Interdependence:

Roles, one paper graded.

Individual Accountability:

Everyone writes, everyone signs in agreement of The Count's paper.

Criteria for Success:

18 – 20 points ······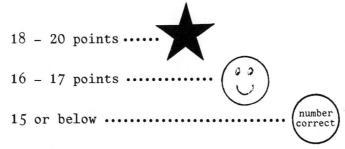

16 – 17 points ············

15 or below ···························

I also will pick someone from your group at random to read or spell or tell the meaning of one of the words. Make sure everyone is prepared to represent your group.

Expected Behaviors:

I expect to see everyone helping, everyone listening carefully to the group members, and everyone doing his or her job.

❧ Monitoring and Processing ❧

Monitoring: Observe each group for short periods of time and record observations on the Teacher Observation Sheet.

Intervening: Intervene if a group needs guidance to ensure participation, agreement, and consideration of each other.

Ending: Give a content check-up quiz, written or oral. If written, pick four words, dictate, match meaning. If oral, choose one child from each group to spell the word dictated and tell the meaning. Or, have children read the word on the board identified by: *Read word number one (or number three, etc.).* If children get stuck, encourage them to get help from their group.

Processing: Give groups one minute to discuss how they did. Then, briefly, have each tell whether their group finished the task and how they felt while working together. Report on how many points the class received in the categories on the Teacher Observation Sheet.

Note: This lesson was reprinted from **Structuring Cooperative Learning: The 1980 Handbook** by Virginia Lyons (Ed.). Edina, MN: Interaction Book Company, 1980.

Cooperative Reasoning in Math

LINDA SKON

Mounds View, MN

Subject Area: Mathematics

Grade Level: Primary

Lesson Summary: Students use arithmetic sentences to solve story problems requiring mathematical reasoning and one or two computations.

Instructional Objectives: Students will gain practice in using arithmetic sentences to solve story problems requiring mathematical reasoning and one or two computations.

Materials:

ITEM	NUMBER NEEDED
Story problem sheet	One per group
Observation sheet	One per group*
Pencil	One per group
Counters or number lines	One per student

*Optional

Time Required: Thirty to forty minutes

∾ Decisions ∽

Group Size: Three (four, if an observer if used)

**Assignment
To Groups:**   Teacher assigned, with one high, one medium, and one low
achieving math student in each group

Roles: One student in a group of four will be the **Observer**. That
student will not participate in solving the story problems,
but will watch the group and tally under the question mark
when students ask questions and tally under the period when
students give information.

≋ The Lesson ∽

Instructional Task:

*I am going to give each of your groups a set of ten story problems.
Someone in your group should be able to read the problems. Your job
is to read each story problem, write a math sentence telling what happened in the story, and then figure out the missing number. You can
use counters or number lines to help you.*

Positive Interdependence:

*I want one set of answers from the group that you helped with and
agree on.*

Individual Accountability:

*When you have finished, each of you should sign your name to your
group's paper. That means that you helped, shared, and understand.*

Criteria for Success:

Your group should try to answer all of the problems correctly. If your group gets 9 or 10 correct, you have done a super job!

Expected Behaviors:

I expect to see all of you helping and all of you sharing. If you don't understand or agree, ask the others in your group to explain that problem again. If you still think they are wrong, explain your answer to them and see if they agree with you.

Explain Observer Role:

I will pick one of you to be the observer of the group. That student will not parti- cipate in solving the story problems, but will watch the group and tally under the question mark when students ask questions and tally under the period when students give information. (Show the students the observation sheet and explain how to use it.)

≈ Monitoring and Processing ≈

Monitoring: Do this with as little interference as possible.

Intervening: Occasionally ask individuals to explain one of their group's answers.

Evaluating and Processing: As a group finishes the task, quickly score the answers. Ask each member of the group if s/he participated and how s/he felt about the task. Then ask the observer to share what s/he noticed about "asking" and "telling" behaviors. in the group. Spend two to three minutes with each group to initiate this procedure until students become skillful at discussing group processes. Give praise and/or rewards to groups that get 9 or 10 correct.

AUTHOR'S NOTE

Evaluate the lesson by determining whether the students met the conditions you set out. Did all or most of the groups solve the story problems correctly? Do you need to teach more on story problems in the future? Also, did the students demonstrate understanding of the cooperative goal structure? What cooperative skills need to be taught in future lessons?

Note: This lesson was reprinted from Structuring Cooperative Learning: The 1979 Handbook by R. Chasnoff (Ed.). Edina, MN: Interaction Book Company, 1979.

Story Problems

1. Jan has 7 balls. She gave 2 to her friend. How many balls does Jan have left?

2. Ted has 3 boats. He got 6 more. How many boats does Ted have now?

3. Kim has 5 hats. Her friend has 2 hats. Who has more hats, Kim or her friend? How many more hats has Kim?

4. Sam has 4 library books. He returned the 4 library books to the library. How many library books does he have now?

5. Don has 4 pennies. He wants to buy a candy bar that costs 9 pennies. How many more pennies does Don need to buy the candy bar?

6. Sue has 6 cookies. She gave 3 cookies away to friends. How many cookies does Sue have left for herself?

7. Jan gave 2 rings to one friend and 3 rings to another. Jan has 4 rings left for herself. How many rings did Jan have to start with before she gave any away?

8. Joe lost 3 pencils. Now he has 6 left. How many pencils did Joe have before losing any?

9. Mom had 10 plates. She broke 4 plates. Mom went out and bought 2 new plates. How many good plates does Mom have now?

10. Bob had 3 pennies. He found 4 more pennies. Then Bob spent 6 pennies. How many pennies does he have now?

Names of Group Members	?	◑

My Name (Observer) _____

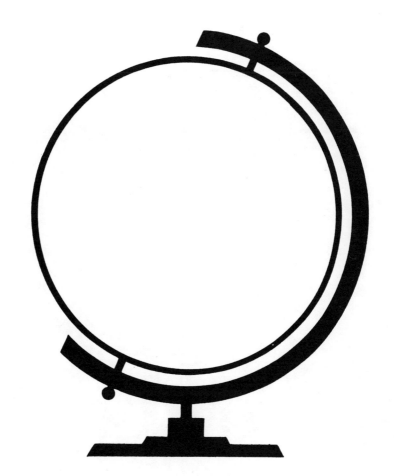

Intermediate

Answering Comprehension Questions
in Reading

ROGER T. JOHNSON

DAVID W. JOHNSON

Minneapolis,
MN

Subject Area: Reading

Grade Level: Elementary

LESSON SUMMARY: Group members read silently, getting help in identifying
words from each other, then summarize together. Members
are given part of the comprehension questions; they
read their questions to the group and write down the
group's best answer. When all three parts of the paper
are completed, it is taped together and signed.

**Instructional
Objectives:**   Students will get practice and help in answering reading
comprehension questions.

Materials:

ITEM	NUMBER NEEDED
Reading Text	One per student
Comprehension Questions	One set per group*
Envelopes	One per student
"How Well Did I Do In Helping My Group?"	One per student
"How Well Did the Group Do?"	One per group

*Each group member receives one-third of the questions in his/her
envelope.

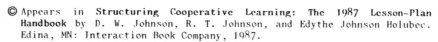

Time Required: From twenty to sixty minutes

≈ Decisions ≈

Group Size: Three

**Assignment
to Groups:**   If all members of the reading group read at about the
same level, form random groups by having the students
count off.   If reading skill variations exist, assign
a high, medium, and low student to each group.

Roles: None

≈ The Lesson ≈

Instructional Task:

*You are to read the story in your book to yourself. Ask your group
members for help if you have trouble with any of the words. When
everyone in the group has finished reading, spend a few minutes summarizing the story out loud together. When you are sure everyone
understands what happened, open your envelopes. They contain the
questions I want you to answer about the story. Each of you is
responsible for reading your questions to the group,
helping the group come up with a good answer for the
questions, and writing the answer to your questions
down. When all three of you have written the
group's answers down, tape your parts together and
sign it.*

Positive Interdependence:

For this assignment, I want you to work cooperatively. You are to help each other read the story and answer the questions. I want just one paper from your group which includes the answers to all your questions.

Individual Accountability:

You are responsible for getting the group to answer the questions in your envelope and for writing the answers down. You are also responsible for helping your group members answer their questions and get them written down. When you sign your group's paper, it means that you agree with all of the answers and can explain why they are correct.

Criteria for Success:

*If you get eight or nine of the nine questions right, you are **fantastic**. Five, six, or seven is **okay**. Below five questions right, you **need to read the story again.***

Expected Behaviors:

I expect to see the following things as I observe the groups:
- *Make sure that all three students get a chance to help.*
- *Listen carefully to each other's ideas.*
- *Say so when you don't understand an answer or question.*
- *Say so when you think someone's idea is good.*

≈ Monitoring and Processing ≈

Monitoring: While the students are working, watch to see how well they are handling the task and how well they are exhibiting the behaviors stressed in setting up the groups. Occasionally, ask a student to explain one of the answers already agreed on and recorded to emphasize the fact that all the group members need to be able to explain the answers. Often, turn students' questions back to the group to solve, or ask students to check with a neighboring group.

Intervening: When a group is obviously struggling, watch for a moment, then intervene. Point out the problem and ask the group what can be done about it. This establishes the teacher's role as one of consultant rather than answer giver. *What is the group going to do about this?* is a useful phrase for you in the cooperative goal structure. You can (and should) suggest possibilities along with the students, sometimes explain a skill, and help the group decide on an effective strategy. Then refocus the group on the task and move on.

Processing: At the end of the lesson, ask each student to fill out the checklist **"How Well Did I Do in Helping My Group?"** Then, have each group discuss the questions on the processing sheet **"How Well Did Our Group Do?"** Finally, lead a discussion on how well the groups worked together. Be careful to model good processing techniques by sticking close to actual observations and stressing positive behaviors. This processing is an important part of the lesson, so always leave time for it.

———————————————

AUTHOR'S NOTE

The first few times cooperative groups are used, it would be wise to have all the student involved, each reading his/her story and answering questions in cooperative groups. This frees you to do the monitoring and skill teaching without having to wonder what the other students are doing. With the whole class involved, it also gives you the opportunity to take a middle-group story and divide the students heterogeneously with a good reader, a middle reader, and a low reader in the same group. This "mix" is a potentially powerful one and a healthy experience for all.

HOW WELL DID I DO
IN HELPING OUR GROUP?

1. I made sure that everyone got a chance to help.

   Yes   Sometimes   No

2. I listened carefully to everyone's ideas.

   Yes   Sometimes   No

3. I said so when I didn't understand
   an answer or question.

   Yes   Sometimes   No

4. I said so when I thought someone's idea was good.

   Yes   Sometimes   No

HOW WELL DID OUR GROUP DO?

1.   We made sure that all of us got a chance to help.

      Yes   Sometimes   No

2.   We listened carefully to each other's ideas.

      Yes   Sometimes   No

3.   We said so when we didn't understand
     an answer or question.

      Yes   Sometimes   No

4.   We said so when we thought someone's
     idea was good.

      Yes   Sometimes   No

Correcting Contraction and Punctuation Errors

SUSAN WHALEN

Greenwich,

CT

Subject Area: Language Arts

Grade Level: Intermediate

Lesson Summary: Students correct the contraction and punctuation mistakes in a letter.

Instructional Objectives: Students will gain practice in correcting contractions and punctuation mistakes in writing.

Materials:

ITEM	NUMBER NEEDED
Letter	One per group
Pencil	One per group
Observation Form	One per group

Time Required: Thirty to thirty-five minutes

≈ Decisions ≈

Group Size: Two

**Assignment
To Groups:**   Teacher assigned, with high- and low-achieving students in each group.

Roles: **Reader:** Reads letter aloud

        Writer: Makes corrections on letter

≈ The Lesson ≈

Instructional Task:

I am going to give you a letter that has a lot of punctuation mistakes in it. Your job will be to read it and correct all the mistakes. You will need to locate the contractions and put in the apostrophes. You will also need to put capital letters and periods and commas where they are needed. (If necessary, review contractions and punctuation rules.)

Positive Interdependence:

You will get one letter and have one pencil, so you will need to make certain you both agree on a correction before it is made. You will hand in one paper and you both will receive the grade from that paper. In addition, both of you will have jobs to do (assign and explain roles).

Individual Accountability:

When you are finished, sign the paper. Remember that your signature means that you agree with the corrections and can explain why you made them to me.

Criteria for Success:

Try to find all of the mistakes. You will be successful if you find all or all but one of the errors.

Expected Behaviors:

I expect to see both of you looking at the letter, both of you agreeing on corrections before the writer makes them, and both of you doing your jobs. In addition, I will be observing for listening, giving ideas, disagreeing nicely, and encouraging others.

≈ Monitoring and Processing ≈

Monitoring: Monitor to make sure that students understand the task and are doing it correctly. Also check to make certain that each student is doing his or her job and that they are agreeing on a correction before the writer marks it.

Intervening: If any pairs are struggling with the task, you may need to reteach some of the information. If they are having trouble working together, you may need to remind them of the expected behaviors.

Processing: Report to each group how they did in working together by showing them the marks on the observation sheet. In addition, have each student tell his or her partner something (besides the job) which they did to help the group.

AUTHOR'S NOTE

Depending on your class, you may want to tell your students how many errors they will find. Also, if your students are not practiced in correcting this kind of assignment, you may want to correct a similar letter as a class to model the assignment.

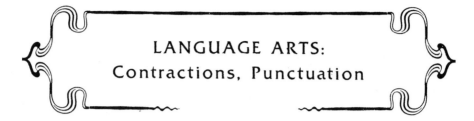

LANGUAGE ARTS:
Contractions, Punctuation

1. Find the contractions in the letter below and **underline them.** You should find six.

2. **Put in** the missing apostrophes, capitals, and periods.

3. **Listen** to your partner. **Say** three or more nice things to each other.

---

dear   steven,

i   cant   decide   what   to   do   this   summer   paul   said   that   hes   going   to   minnesota   eric   might   go   to   camp   ive   heard   that   katie   and   michelle   will   take   swimming   lessons   emily   doesn't   know   what   shes   going   to   do   i   guess   ill   have   to   think   about   this   a   lot!   come   on   over   to   my   house   and   help   me   decide

your   friend,

michael

Sign your names here when you are certain you have made all the corrections and that both of you can explain them:

_____

_____

➤ **OBSERVATION SHEET** ➤

	Group Members	
Listens		
Gives Ideas		
Disagrees Nicely		
Encourages Others		

Other Behaviors Observed:

Book Report Roulette

GLADY LAUGHLIN

Las Vegas,
NV

Subject Area: Language Arts

Grade Level: Intermediate

Lesson Summary: Students sign a contract to read a book or books. When they are ready, they report to their group and follow the format of **Book Report Roulette**.

Instructional Objectives: Students will increase their reading comprehension through independent reading, will increase higher level thinking skills through discussion of reading materials, and will enhance their oral language and social skills through working in groups.

Materials:

ITEM	NUMBER NEEDED
Book Report Roulette Rules	One per student
Book Report Contract	One per student
Book Report Questions	One per group
Book Report Roulette Record Sheet	One per group
Game Boards	One set per group
Dice	One pair per group
Students' novels	Student choice

Time Required: Fifteen minutes for initial instructions; forty-five minutes a week, every week, for the game.

≈ Decisions ≈

Group Size: Three or more students in each group

**Assignment
To Groups:**   Teacher assigned, with a heterogeneous mix: high/medium/low, male/female, racial, and mainstreamed students together.

Roles: **Reporter:** Person telling about book

Encourager: Person who asks clarifying questions and maintains eye contact with the Reporter

Scribe: Person who completes record sheet

(Additional roles of **Noise Monitor**, **Summarizer**, and/or Observer may be used as needed.)

≈ The Lesson ≈

Instructional Task:

Prior to reporting day: Assign students the responsibility of reading books, explain the rules and responsibilities of **Book Report Roulette**, and have students read their contracts and have them signed.

Reporting Day: *Let's go over the rules for the game: The Reporter shakes the dice and answers the question on the appropriate game board which corresponds to the number on the dice. The Encourager's job is to ask additional questions as needed to get a satisfactory answer. When the group has determined that enough information has been given to answer the question, the Scribe records the group's response on the Report Sheet.*

Repeat this procedure until three or more questions are answered. If the Reporter rolls a repeat number, s/he rolls again until s/he gets a new number. If the Reporter's answers are not satisfactory, the game ends and the Reporter must try again another time. Only one more try is allowed on the same book. Rotate reports until everyone in the group has reported on their books.

Positive Interdependence:

Books cannot be reported on without the group. There will be one report from the group, and all members must perform their roles in order to complete the report.

Individual Accountability:

Each person must do h/her job in order to complete the task. The Reporter is accountable for knowing h/her book. The Encourager is accountable for getting good answers from the Reporter, and the Scribe is accountable for writing the Reporter's (and group's) final answers.

Criteria for Success:

You are successful if you read and successfully report on books from all three categories. The groups are successful if they turn in completed reports from each group member and the answers they approve are of high quality. (For a nine-week period with my sixth-graders, I used the following grading: six books = C; seven books = B; and eight books = A.)

Expected Behaviors:

The Reporter's job is to report fully on h/her books. The other members' jobs are to help the Reporter do this. So, I expect each of you to do your job in the group, and I expect to hear lots of encouraging and lots of clarifying questions or comments.

～ Monitoring and Processing ～

Monitoring: Observe the groups to listen for information that should be asked for, to see if students are doing their jobs correctly, and to gather information on groups and individuals working well together to report to the class.

Intervening: If necessary, intervene to teach question-asking or social skills. For example, ask the group members for ways they can ask questions about ideas, then model for the students good ways to ask questions. Also, make sure when they criticize that they maintain the focus on ideas and don't criticize people.

Processing: Have the students write on the back of the Record Sheet what each one said to encourage or clarify. Then share with each group what you heard during your monitoring. End by telling the whole class something that you really liked that you observed that day.

AUTHOR'S NOTE

My students loved this game and my greatest problem was to get them to stop asking questions about the books being reported on. They also had to learn to budget their time during the nine weeks so that they didn't have all the book reports due at the end of class. I also had some mainstreamed special education students; I adjusted for them the number of books and pages they had to read, but they still had to answer the questions about their books. I found that they succeeded well with the support that the group gave them in asking questions and writing the report.

Contract

I, _____, do hereby agree to read _____ books and report on them for the grade of _____. I further agree to use books of at least 150 pages. I understand that books of substantially more than 150 pages may count for more than one report if I obtain prior written approval from the teacher and attach that approval slip to the record sheet when my book is reported.

I hereby agree to participate in the group when I am not reporting. I will follow all the rules for cooperative learning groups.

Finally, I agree to use books read only since _____ (date) and complete this contract by _____ (date). I will return this contract, signed by the appropriate parties, within one week of the date it is written.

_____
Student

_____
Parent

_____
Teacher

Book Report Roulette Rules

MATERIALS: Appropriate Roulette Wheel

One pair of dice

Record Sheet

The book of your choice

RULES:

1. Write your Book Report Contract.

2. Have it signed by your parent, teacher and self.

3. Choose and read books from all three categories. They must be at least 150 pages in length unless you receive prior approval from the teacher. (With prior approval, books of substantially more than 150 pages may count as more than one report. The teacher's approval note must be attached to the record sheet.)

4. During Roulette Time, you may report on a completed book in the following manner: Roll the dice and answer the correspondingly numbered question from the appropriate topic wheel. Your group will decide if the question has been answered to their satisfaction. If not, they may ask you for more information. You must answer 3 questions for each book report value. You may bring a book back only once if it is not approved in the first session you report it.

5. The group scribe must complete the **Book Report Roulette** record sheet and submit it to the teacher after each session.

6. You must participate in the group if you do not have a report.

7. When all in your group have reported, you may return to the independent reading.

8. Students with more than one book to report in a session must allow each other group member to play before they do a second or third report.

9. All reports must be completed within the time stated on the contract.

10. If you roll doubles, **except double 1,** answer question 1.

Book Report Roulette Questions

NOVEL/BIOGRAPHY/AUTOBIOGRAPHY

1. Identify the problem in your book.

2. What goal would you like to reach if you had the same problem as the main character?

3. What was the resolution of the problem?

4. Is the publication date the same time setting as the plot? How would the story be changed if it were written in a different time?

5. Is the location of this story the only place it could occur? Why or why not?

6. Is everything in the story believable? Does it need to be?

7. Is any character in the story someone you would choose for a friend? Why or why not?

8. What are the characteristics of the least likable character? Why do you see the character as the least likable?

9. Choose your favorite scene in the story and explain what happened.

10. Why do you think the author wrote this book?

11. If you could change the ending, what would you do?

12. Which character in the book most reminds you of yourself and why?

NONFICTION/FACT

1. Why did you choose this book to read? Explain.

2. Does the author have credibility in this field? Why?

3. Is there information in this book that may be opinion? Explain.

4. If you wanted to know more about a fact in this book, what subject(s) in the card catalog would you look for?

5. Where did the author get his/her information?

6. What information in this book would you like to know more about? Why?

7. If your book has pictures or illustrations, are they well-chosen to explain the written material? Why or why not?

8. What piece of information did you find most interesting? Why?

9. How would you use what you learned in this book?

10. Under what general category would this book fall?

11. Would your book appeal to any other age group? What ages and why do you think as you do?

12. How would you re-name the book?

POETRY

1. What was your favorite poem and why?

2. Read orally the poem that best illustrates the title of the book. Explain why you think this poem describes the title.

3. If you could write a poem about one of the topics in this book, what would you choose and why?

4. Would you read more poems by this author? Why?

    or

    By which poet would you like to read more works? Why?

5. Choose a particularly descriptive set of at least 5 lines. Read them to your group and explain why you chose them.

6. Why was this group of poems published in one book?

7. Choose a poem you would like to illustrate. Explain how you would do it and why.

8. What are the most effective words used by the poet in your favorite poem? Why do you like them?

9. Give an example of alliteration.

10. Give an example of onomatopoeia.

11. Give an example of a simile or a metaphor.

12. Which poem illustrates best how you think or feel about the subject it deals with? Explain.

Book Report Roulette Record Sheet

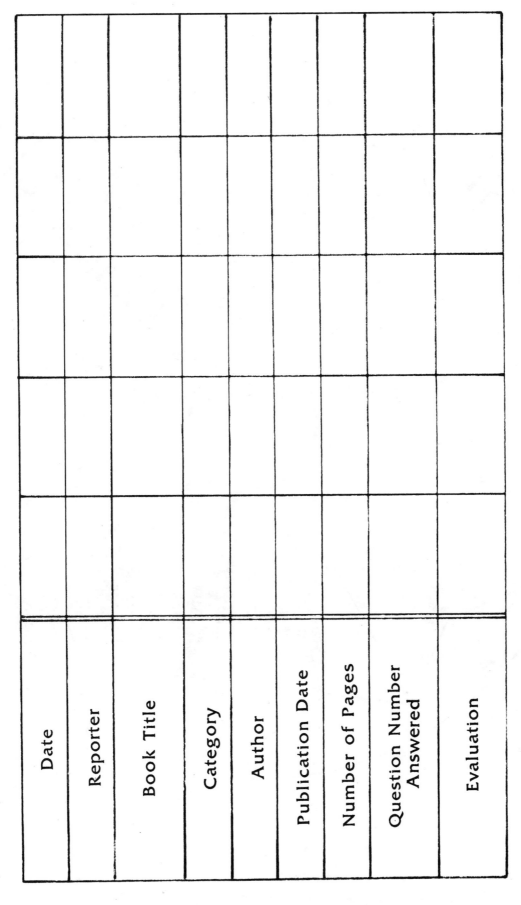

Date	Reporter	Book Title	Category	Author	Publication Date	Number of Pages	Question Number Answered	Evaluation

Additional Comments:

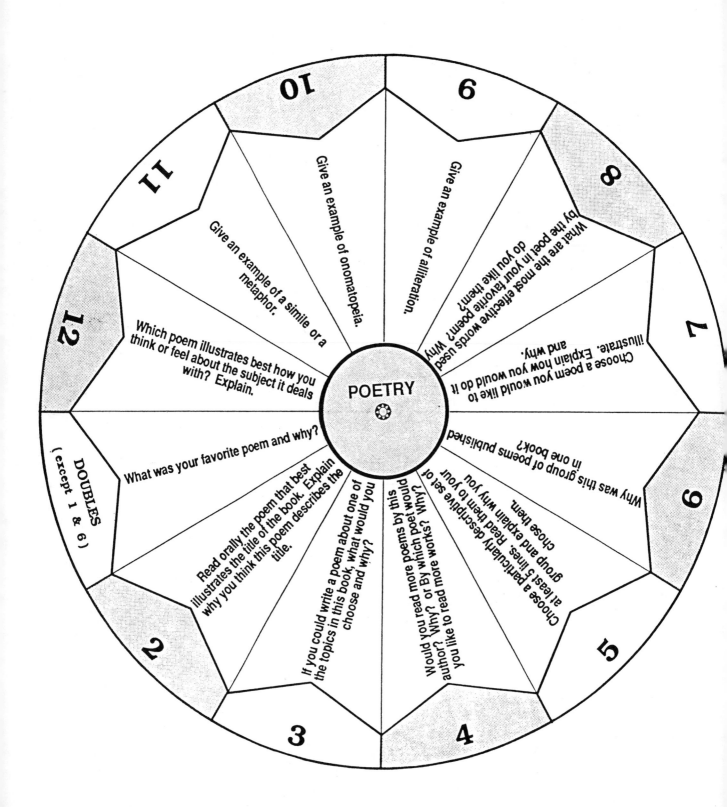

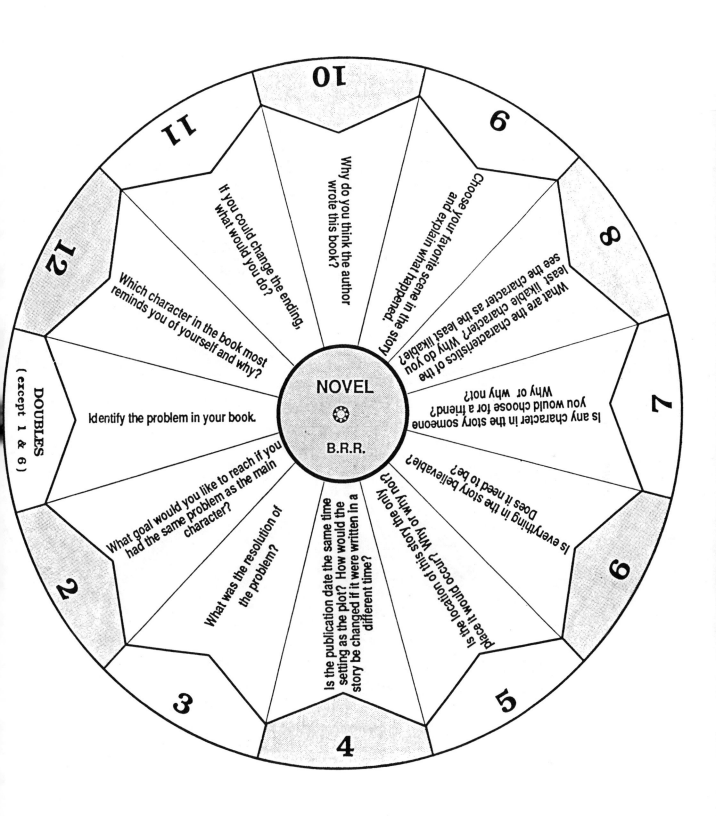

Why do you think the author wrote this book?

Choose your favorite scene in the story and explain what happened.

What are the characteristics of the least likable character? Why do you see the character as the least likable?

Is any character in the story someone you would choose for a friend? Why or why not?

Is everything in the story believable? Does it need to be?

Is the location of this story the only place it would occur? Why or why not?

Is the publication date the same time setting as the plot? How would the story be changed if it were written in a different time?

What was the resolution of the problem?

What goal would you like to reach if you had the same problem as the main character?

Identify the problem in your book.

Which character in the book most reminds you of yourself and why?

If you could change the ending, what would you do?

DOUBLES (except 1 & 6)

NOVEL

B.R.R.

10

9

8

7

6

5

4

3

2

11

12

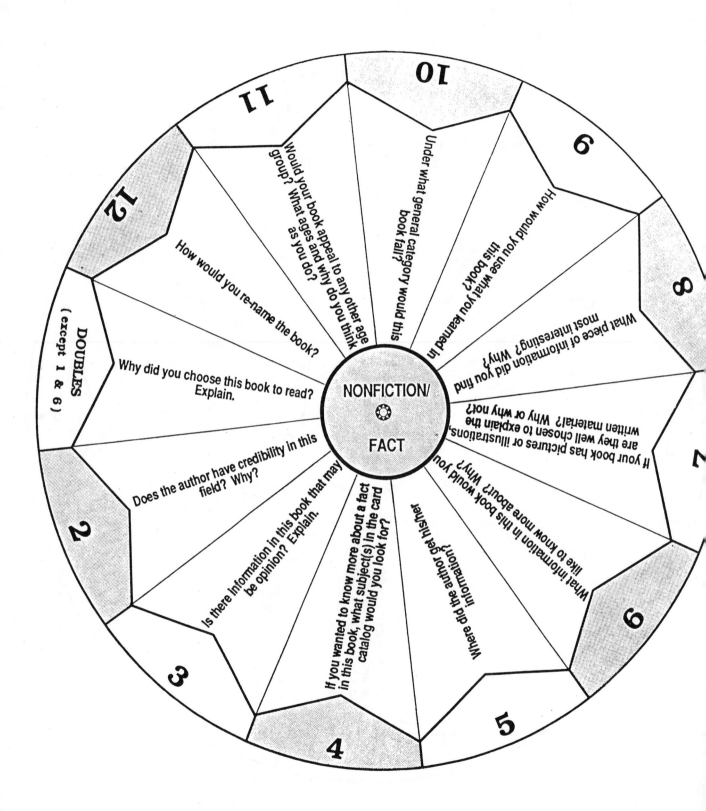

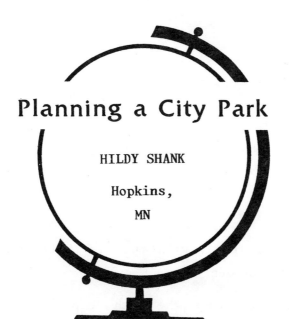

Planning a City Park

HILDY SHANK

Hopkins,

MN

Subject Area: Math; Science

Grade Level: Intermediate

Lesson Summary: Students develop a plan for a city park, create a design, then prepare and present to the class a commercial to sell their park.

**Instructional
  Objectives:**   Students will get practice in planning a large community project while staying within a maximum cost.

Materials:

ITEM	NUMBER NEEDED
The Task*	One per group
Materials and Cost Worksheet	One per group
16" x 20" piece of tagboard	One per group
Set of role cards	One per group

*Adapted from **S.P.A.C.E.S.**, Dale Seymour Publications, Palo Alto, California, 1982.

Time Required: Three class periods, each one week apart

≈ Decisions ≈

Group Size: Four

Assignment To Groups: Teacher assigned, with one high, two medium, and one low achieving student in each group.

Roles: **Accountant:** Does the math computations and records the group's final report.

Architect: Lays out the park on the piece of tagboard.

Encourager: Makes sure every group member is participating.

Manager: Reads the instructions for the activity, reports the group's plan and its cost to the whole class at the end of the period, and leads the processing discussion for the group at the end of the second day.

≈ The Lesson ≈

Instructional Task:

Day 1: Your task will be to build a park for the city of Golden Valley, Minnesota (read Task Sheet). You are to plan the design of 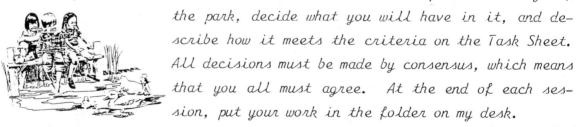 the park, decide what you will have in it, and describe how it meets the criteria on the Task Sheet. All decisions must be made by consensus, which means that you all must agree. At the end of each session, put your work in the folder on my desk.

Day 2: Today you are to take your ideas for the playground and lay them out on a 16 x 20-inch piece of tagboard. Include somewhere in the park five trees, one hill, an outcropping of rocks, and one stream. You must decide where each natural feature goes. Keep the same roles you had last time. At the end of the class, the group manager will report your plan to the class. Then you will process how well you worked together.

Day 3: Today your task is to (1) finish your plans for the park, (2) write a report explaining why your park has the design it has, (3) write a commercial to sell your park to the rest of the class, and (4) present your commercial to the class, with all group members participating in it. After that, we will vote as a class, using secret ballots, for which park is best and why.

Positive Interdependence:

I want one plan from your group that you all agree upon, each of you must perform your roles to help the group get the task done, and you all must plan and take part in the commercial.

Individual Accountability:

Each of you will be given a role which is essential to the group's work. In order to complete your park plan, every member has to fulfill his or her responsibility.

Criteria for Success:

Your group is successful if you build a park plan which all members agree upon and which meets the cost requirement, if your written report is clear, and if your commercial is convincing.

Expected Behaviors:

I expect to see you all working and helping, and all of you performing your assigned roles. If you have problems agreeing, try to solve those problems in your group.

∼ Monitoring and Processing ∼

Monitoring: Observe the groups during the lesson, giving advice and answering questions when needed. When you see students behaving skillfully, praise and reinforce the use of those skills. Also, collect information on students who use group skills effectively to report during the whole-class processing.

Intervening: If any groups have difficulties in working together or making decisions which they cannot solve, intervene to help them come to a satisfactory conclusion.

Processing: At the end of the second session, the Manager conducts a group discussion on what members did to work effectively with each other and what they can do to improve their working together. Each group's answers are written down and turned in with their work. Then, ask groups to report a few of their answers to the whole class, and report on the group skills you saw effectively used.

AUTHOR'S NOTE

I really like the feeling of pride and success that this lesson produces in my students. They typically feel that they have fully used their abilities in producing a quality park plan. I also believe that students need the experience of analyzing how well they are working together so they can plan how to improve, put their plans into action, and feel pride and success when the group functions better.

A footnote to this lesson is that, after hearing about it, the P.T.A. gave our class $3,000 to buy new equipment for the school playground. Each group will make a plan of how the playground should function, what new equipment is needed, and where it should be placed. The groups will present their plan to the P.T.A., which will adopt the one it likes the best.

GOLDEN VALLEY PARK

The Task

Golden Valley has decided to develop some of its land as an environmental park. Your engineering team has been asked to submit a proposal for the development of this land. The people of the town will do the work. Your team will plan what materials and equipment will be needed. The total cost of these materials and equipment must be $5,000 or less. Consider the following criteria when developing your plan:

VERSATILITY:

- Is the park suitable (meets the needs) for the elderly, the young, and the in-between?
- Can the park be used at night as well as during the day?
- Is the park useful in all seasons?
- Is there a wide range of activities available within the park?

SAFETY:

- How safe is the design for young and old users?
- Are there any possible hazards?

AESTHETICS:

- Is the design pleasing?
- Would people of all ages enjoy the park?

COST EFFECTIVENESS:

- Was the money well spent?
- Is energy used efficiently in the park?

INNOVATION:

- Is the design unusual?
- Are materials used in new and interesting ways?

COST OF MATERIALS AND EQUIPMENT

	Cost	Unit	Quantity	Total Cost
Rope	$1	per 10′		
Bricks	$1	each		
Sand	$1	cubic foot		
Stepping stones	$5	each		
Plants and shrubs	$10	each		
Trash barrels	$10	each		
Benches (6′ long)	$15	each		
Old telephone poles (10′ long)	$25	each		
Wire fencing (6′ high)	$30	per 10 running feet		
Asphalt pavement (4′ wide)	$40	per 10 running feet		
Picnic tables with two benches	$50	each		
Community garden plot and seedlings	$50	10′ × 10′		
Animals Small . . . . Large	$20 $100	each each		
Drinking fountains	$75	each		
Pond	$100	each		
Playground equipment	$100	per item		
Bike racks	$150	each		
Barbeques	$150	each		
Street lights	$250	each		
Public telescope	$300	each		
Stage (20′ square)	$300	each		
Bathrooms (one each, men and women) . . .	$350	pair		
Bleachers (grandstand)	$750	each		
Bridge	$1000	each		
Other (list)	$			
	$			

TOTAL COST: $ _____

Solve the Mystery Melody

DR. SUSAN R. SNYDER

Greenwich,
CT

Subject Area: Music

Grade Level: Intermediate

Lesson Summary: Information on playing part of a melody on resonator bells will be given to each group, with each member receiving part of the information necessary to figure out and play its part. If the groups are successful, the class will be able to recognize the melody it plays.

**Instructional
Objectives:** Students will be able to play a phrase of **Greensleeves** on resonator bells by decoding the phrases' notation.

Materials:

ITEM	NUMBER NEEDED
Instruction sheet sets	One per group
Pencils	One per group
Resonator bell sets	One per group
Mallets	One per student

※ Appropriate pitches for the group's melodic segment

Time Required: Thirty minutes

≈ Decisions ≈

Group Size: Four members per group.   If the class does not divide evenly into fours, one member of some groups could assume two roles, for example, the **Master Plan Holder** could combine with the **Clue Master.**

**Assignment
To Groups:**   Post the numbers 1-6 at stations around the room.   Each page of directions has a group number on it; shuffle the pages and pass them out.   After all the pages have been distributed, have students proceed to the station matching the group number on their page.

Roles: **Master Plan Holder**
                 Key Master   (These roles are explained on the
                 Clue Master   attached handouts)
                 Bell Master

Observer: The teacher is the observer, and should carry an observation sheet which lists the interaction goals of following directions in sequential order and listening carefully to group members.

≈ The Lesson ≈

Instructional Task:

Your job will be to play a phrase of a melody on the bells, based on information your group receives.

Positive Interdependence:

Each person in the group will receive only a part of the information necessary to complete this task; each group will receive only part of the melody which makes up the song.

Individual Accountability:

You will need to read the sheet you receive, learn your material, and teach your material to your group members.

Criteria for Success:

Ten minutes before the end of class I will ask your group to play your phrase of the melody on the resonator bells. As each group plays its phrase in sequence, you should be able to recognize the melody.

Expected Behaviors:

I expect to see you following the directions on your sheet in sequential order, asking for help if you need it, and listening carefully to your group members.

∼ Monitoring and Processing ∼

Monitoring: Observe how the groups are working together and how well they are following the sequence described on the Master Plan Holder's page. One indication will be how quickly the Bell Master comes to claim the bells. Mark specific interaction comments on the Observation Sheet, including groups and group members working well, groups and group members with problems to be solved, and interaction issues needing attention in the future.

Intervening: Assist groups in following the sequence and in working together when necessary. Assist only as needed. The design of the master pages, as well as the need for active involvement, builds in the interdependence of all group members.

Ending: As each group finishes the task, listen to its portion of the melody. Check to see that all four group members are playing at least one bell. Check understanding of the notation on the Clue Master's page by pointing to a given note and asking the Bell Master to describe how he or she knows that the letter name under the note is correct. Have the groups play the melodies in sequential order from one to six and let them discover that the melody is **Greensleeves**.

Processing: Discuss any general observations about student interaction, then ask for comments about what worked well and what changes could be made to improve cooperation of group members. Limit the discussion to the social skills of listening and following directions in sequential order.

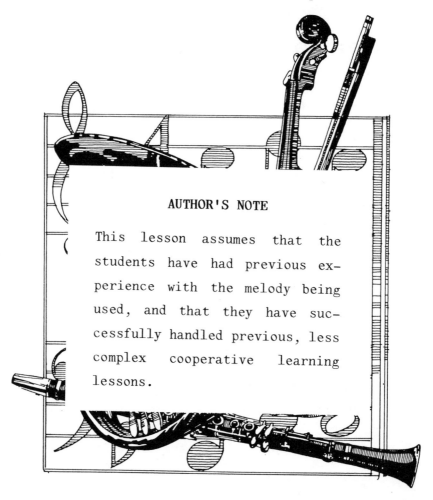

AUTHOR'S NOTE

This lesson assumes that the students have had previous experience with the melody being used, and that they have successfully handled previous, less complex cooperative learning lessons.

MASTER PLAN HOLDER ♪ Group ___

Read these directions to your group, one at a time. If they are followed in order, your group will succeed in solving the mystery.

DIRECTION 1: Each person read your directions silently. If you can't read a word, ask a group member for help.

DIRECTION 2: Key Master: Read your information to the group. Be sure everyone understands the information.

DIRECTION 3: Clue Master: Read your information to the group. Fill in the letter names on your paper as we tell them to you, one at a time.

DIRECTION 4: Bell Master: Read your page to the group all the way through, then follow the directions, one step at a time.

When the group finishes the task, each member should sign below.

Master Plan Holder _____

Bell Master _____

Key Master _____

Clue Master _____

KEY

MASTER   Group ____

You hold the key to solving your group's piece of the puzzle.

Read this information to your group:

Every line and every space on the staff has a letter name. When a note is on that line or space, it tells you to play that letter name. Here are the names:

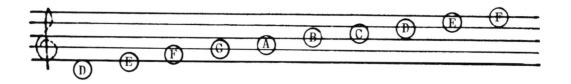

The spaces spell F A C E.
The lines are E G B D F.

Everyone in your group should understand this information before you go on. How are you sure everyone understands this? You may need to have each group member point to a few notes as you say the letter names.

You need a pencil to do this job.

The **Key Master** will tell you the names of the lines and spaces.

Write the letter names under each of the notes below as the group members

    tell them to you.

(PLACE INDIVIDUAL GROUP'S CLUE HERE)

Now listen to the **Bell Master**. You will need to help. This paper will

    be needed.

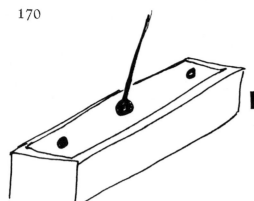

BELL MASTER

Group _____

Read all these directions to your group, then follow them one step at a time.

- After you have completed the Clue Master paper, get your bell set from the teacher.

- The **Bell Master** will give each person in the group at least one bell and one mallet. Some people in the group may be given more than one bell.

- Play the melody on the **Clue Master's** paper by each playing your bell when the letter name appears in the melody.

- Make it sound like a song you know.

The melodic segments to be inserted on each **Clue Master's** page are as follows:

The bells to be organized for each group (I put them in baskets marked with the group number) are:

Group 1:	E	G	A	B	C
Group 2:	D	E	F#	A	
Group 3:	low B	D#	E	F	G
Group 4:	E	G	A	B	C
Group 5:	D	E	F#	A	
Group 6:	C#	D#	E	F#	G

Cooperative Computers

DIANE BROWNE

Hopkins,

MN

Subject Area: Language Arts; Computers

Grade Level: Intermediate

Lesson Summary: Students correct capitalization, punctuation, spelling, and language errors in a paragraph and also on the computer.

Instructional Objectives:

1. Every student will be able to recognize the errors and make the necessary corrections in the paragraph.
2. Every student will know how to use the word processor to make corrections on the computer.

Materials:

ITEM	NUMBER NEEDED
Paragraph to proofread	One per student
Paragraph on computer disk	One per group
Theme paper	One per student
Group Process worksheet	One per group
Computer	One per group

Time Required: One class period

≈ Decisions ≈

Group Size: Four

**Assignment
To Groups:**   Teacher assigned, with a high, two medium, and one low achieving student in each group.

Roles: **Manager:**   Makes sure each person participates; identifies and changes capitalization errors.

Checker: Checks to make sure the group is in agreement with the changes and that everyone knows how to make the corrections on the computer; identifies and changes punctuation errors.

Recorder: Passes out the materials; collects, checks over, and turns in assignments; identifies and changes spelling errors.

Processor: Observes group members working, gives positive feedback, discusses answers and records on **Group Processing** worksheet; identifies and changes language errors.

≈ The Lesson ≈

Instructional Task:

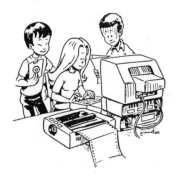

Your job will be to proofread a paragraph together, discussing the errors and possible corrections, and giving reasons for any changes you recommend. When you all agree on a correction, the student whose job it is to make that type of correction will make it on the worksheet and on the computer. When you are finished, each of you will rewrite the paragraph on theme paper.

Positive Interdependence:

You need to take turns finding errors. One of you will look for capitalization, one for punctuation, one for spelling, and one for language. Make certain you all agree before anyone makes any changes. Make certain also that you all know how to make the corrections on the computer and make them correctly. Only the person whose job it is can make that correction.

Individual Accountability:

Each of you has a job to do and a role to perform to help the group function. I will collect one of the four theme papers from the group to grade.

Criteria for Success:

I will grade the computer printout. Then if the paragraph I choose has 90% accuracy or more, your group will receive four bonus points; 80 - 89% will earn you three bonus points; 70 - 79% will get two bonus points; 60 - 69% will get one bonus point. Below 50% accuracy, your group must redo the assignment. (Teachers may want to vary the grading.)

≈ Monitoring and Processing ≈

Monitoring: Watch to make sure that each member is performing his or her group role. Give informal feedback on how well the groups are working while you are observing.

Intervening: Intervene when necessary to help students with the task or help them perform their roles.

Processing: Have students discuss, complete, and turn in the Group Process Worksheet.

FIND the ERRORS

A fable is a story that is up made to Teach a lesson. animals behave like beings human in many fabels. Some are wise. Others are stuped. The the sly fox the carefree grasshopper and the vain crow are characters in fables that are known in mamy country.

A greek slave named aesop wrote many of the fables more than twenty five hundred years ago. Isn't it it remarkable that we can still enjoy them.

Note: If this worksheet is correctly worked, there will be sixteen errors indicated.

GROUP PROCESSING

What skills were you practicing?

_____
_____

Names of participants   Roles

1 _____   _____
2 _____   _____
3 _____   _____
4 _____   _____

What did your group accomplish?

_____
_____
_____

What helped you get it done?

_____
_____

What got in your way? _____

_____

Volleyball Skill Practice

NANCY KILLGORE

Snohomish,

WA

Subject Area: Physical Education

Grade Level: Fourth and up

Instructional Objectives: To practice a new volleyball skill within the framework of cooperative pairs.

Materials:

ITEM	NUMBER NEEDED
Volleyballs	One per group

Time Required: One class period

≈ Decisions ≈

Group Size: Two

Assignment To Groups: Random, by counting off

Roles: None

≈ The Lesson ≈

Opening Game:

Beach Ball Boogie: This is a pair game where students exchange the ball from one set of partners to another without using their hands.

Exercises:

I start with a period of timed jogging with students paired and only one member of the pair is running at a time. The goal is to continue running the entire time, taking turns with your partner and spelling one another as the other gets tired.

Lesson Core:

Volleyball Skill: Volleying: First, I instruct students on how to perform a "volley" correctly. Then they practice with one partner tossing to the other while the other volleys back, then they switch roles. After that, they practice volleying continually back and forth with their partner. Next, they practice volleying off a wall with the partner standing behind to retrieve the ball if necessary, count the number done in succession, and encourage the partner. When they have had adequate practice, I add 30-second timing to the wall volley activity: This is where partners trade volleying every 30 seconds and turn in accumulative scores for both of them. Finally, students practice volleying back and forth over the net with their partners.

Closing Activity:

Game: Volley Newcomb: Partners take opposite sides of the net to form two teams. Points are scored for each legal volley. Serves are alternated between teams. Partners keep track of the total number of points they score together.

Processing:

Tell the students things you noticed which reinforce their working together well. Have students tell their partners something they did which helped them today and then suggest they thank their partner for helping.

*Note: This lesson was adapted from one found in **The Second Cooperative Sports and Games Book** by Terry Orlick. New York: Pantheon Books, 1982.

Junior High

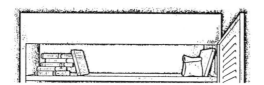

English Comprehension and Composition

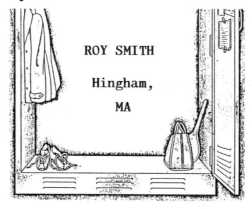

ROY SMITH

Hingham,

MA

Subject Area: English

Grade Level: Junior and Senior High

Lesson Summary: Students read, discuss, and write some of their ideas and feelings about knowing the future. For pre-reading, students brainstorm ideas and write a letter. They read and discuss the story **The Choice**, then write an essay about it. Peer editing is done on the writings.

Instructional Objectives: Students will get practice in four language-arts processes: reading, writing, speaking, and listening.

Materials:

ITEM	NUMBER NEEDED
Pre-reading activity sheet	One per student
Copy of **The Choice***	One per student
Post-reading activity sheet	One per student
Set of role cards	One per group
Group Behavior checklist	One per student
Observation sheet	One per group

**_The Choice_ by Wayland Young. Variations Literature Program, <u>Shadowbox Anthology</u>, Harcourt, Brace & Jovanovich, 1975.

  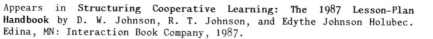

© Appears in **Structuring Cooperative Learning: The 1987 Lesson-Plan Handbook** by D. W. Johnson, R. T. Johnson, and Edythe Johnson Holubec. Edina, MN: Interaction Book Company, 1987.

Time Required: From two to four class sessions

≈ Decisions ≈

Group Size: Four

**Assignment
To Groups:**   Teacher assigned, with high, medium, and low students
and males and females in each group.

Roles: **Encourager of Participation:**   In a friendly way encourages all members of the group to participate in the
discussion, sharing their ideas and feelings.   This
group member also serves as **Reader** who reads assignments and **The Choice** to the group.

Praiser: Compliments group members who do their
assigned work and contribute to the learning of group
members.

Summarizer: Restates the ideas and feelings expressed
in the discussions whenever it is appropriate.   Also,
this group member is the **Recorder** who records the
answers on the two pre-writing activities.

Checker: Makes certain group members have read and
edited the two compositions and that they understand
the general principles of writing.   Collects the group
members' pre-reading and post-reading compositions,
staples them together, then hands them in to the
teacher.

≈ The Lesson ≈

Instructional Task:

How would you feel about going into the future? What do you think you would see?   What would you want to tell others about?   Your task will be to do some thinking, reading, and writing about going into the future. To do this, you will work together in coop- erative groups to help each other come up with good ideas, help each other write high-quality, thoughtful, and letter-perfect essays, and help each other understand and think about a story. Specific instruc- tions for each assignment will be given with the assignment sheets.

Positive Interdependence:

*For the pre-writing activities, I want one paper from the group. For the writing activities, I want one paper from each group member, but no one is finished individually until all members of your group are done.   You will read and edit at least two other compositions and make certain that everyone in your group understands the basic principles of writing. When you are certain that your group's papers are perfect, give them to the **Checker** who will collect them, staple them together, and hand them in.*

Individual Accountability:

I must see each of you participating in the discussions and you must be able to defend and explain your group's answers orally when I ask you individually. You will write two thesis essays and revise them to meet the standards of your groupmates. You will sign your name to the essays you edit, certifying that they are as correct as you can help make them and that the group members understand the corrections.

Criteria for Success:

*All students will receive the same grade as their group. Two grades will be given for each set of papers: (1) **Content** -- what you say and how well you say it; and (2) **Mechanics** -- how correct the papers are in terms of complete sentences, unified paragraphs, punctuation, spelling, and English usage. For mechanics, if there are no errors, the group will receive an "A." One to five errors will be a "B." Six to ten errors will be a "C." Eleven to fifteen errors will be a "D." More than fifteen errors will be an "F." The group discussion papers will be checked but not graded.* (Teachers may want to set their own criteria for the grading of the compositions.)

Expected Behaviors:

I expect to see all of you helping your group members, listening carefully to them, participating in all your assignments, and pushing each other to do perfect work. If you are absent, make certain you telephone a group member and get the assignment done.

Roles Assigned:

Each group will get a set of role cards. Pass them out randomly each day and make certain you understand and are prepared to perform your role for the day. I will be observing for those four roles plus **Asking for Help, Giving Help, and Criticizing Constructively.** (Show students your observation sheet and make certain they understand the roles.)

≈ Monitoring and Processing ≈

Monitoring: While the groups work, unobtrusively observe for deficits in both English and cooperative skills. Give help where you think it is needed,

respond to students' questions, but, whenever feasible, turn the questions back to the group members to answer. Occasionally, randomly pick a student from a group to explain some aspect of writing. This is to remind students that, besides turning in correct compositions, all members must understand how to read and write effectively. Also, look for good examples of group skills and praise the groups for them. Spend about five to ten minutes formally observing each group with the observation sheet.

Intervening: When a group has a problem in mastering some aspect of reading and writing that they obviously cannot solve, intervene to teach them the needed English skills. When a group has a problem in working together that they obviously cannot solve, intervene to teach them better cooperative skills.

Processing: During the last five or ten minutes of each class period, students should process their effectiveness in working together. On various days, have individuals fill out the Student Checklist and give the groups your completed Observation Sheets so they can answer the following questions:

1.   *What did we do well as a group today?*

2.   *What could we do even better tomorrow?*

AUTHOR'S NOTE

Students working in cooperative learning groups have an opportunity to engage in four language arts processes: **reading, writing, speaking,** and **listening.** Students working individually can only do the first two, and then not as efficiently. Discussion, involving speaking and listening, enables students to collect ideas, try them out, and revise them before committing them to paper. Cooperative groups produce higher levels of cognitive reasoning and analysis than do individuals working alone. More effective learning is the result.

⟶⟩⟩⟨ PREREADING ACTIVITY: <u>The Choice</u> by Wayland Young ⟩⟨⟨⟵

1. **PREWRITING:** *As a group, list as many ideas as you can for each of the following topics. Do not criticize or evaluate each other's ideas and make sure every member contributes some ideas for each topic. Be creative and build on each other's ideas.*

    a. If you were to travel into the future, what would you take with you?

    b. If you were to travel into the future, what would you want to find out?

    c. If you were to travel into the future, what would you plan to tell others about what you observed?

2. **WRITING:** *Working by yourself, write a letter on the topic described below. When you are finished, have the other members of your group read the letter and make suggestions on how it may be improved. While they are doing so, read the letters of all the other group members and give them your comments on how their letters may be improved. The topic is as follows:*

> You want to be the first "time-traveler" in the world, but you need someone to finance the trip. Write a letter to the well-known financier, John W. Davidson, to try and persuade him to provide the money for the trip. In your letter, explain that you want to be the first time-traveler. Also explain your plans for observing the future and reporting the results to the present members of your society. Include the three topics listed in the prewriting activity and anything else about traveling into the future you think is important. Provide as much detail as possible.

POSTREADING ACTIVITY: The Choice by Wayland Young

1. **PREWRITING:**   *In your group, discuss the following questions without referring back to the story.   Write down at least three answers for each question and then circle the one that the group likes the best.*

    a.   How long did Williams' friend have to wait before Williams returned?

    b.   What did Williams remember from his trip?

    c.   How did Williams feel about his choice?

    d.   Why do you suppose Williams made the choice he did?

    e.   Why weren't the camera, notebook, and recorder used?

    f.   What reasons would you give for calling Williams brave?

    What reasons would you give for calling Williams a coward?

    In your opinion, was Williams a cowardly or brave person?

    g.   What important techniques did the author use in writing this story?

2. **WRITING:**   *Working by yourself, write a theme on the topic described below. When you are finished, have the other members of your group read the theme and make suggestions on how it may be improved.   While they are doing so, read the themes of all the other group members and give them your comments on how their themes may be improved. The topic is as follows:*

    Pretend you are a lawyer preparing to argue before the Supreme Court.   Williams is being tried to determine whether or not his decision was a correct one.   Look at the arguments for both sides (in prewriting).   Decide whether he was right or wrong and write a paper (lawyers call it a brief) to be submitted to the Court for consideration in the decision-making process by the judges.   Your paper should first state your decision (position).   Then state your reasons (defense for your position).   Each reason should be explained in as much detail as possible.

OBSERVATION SHEET

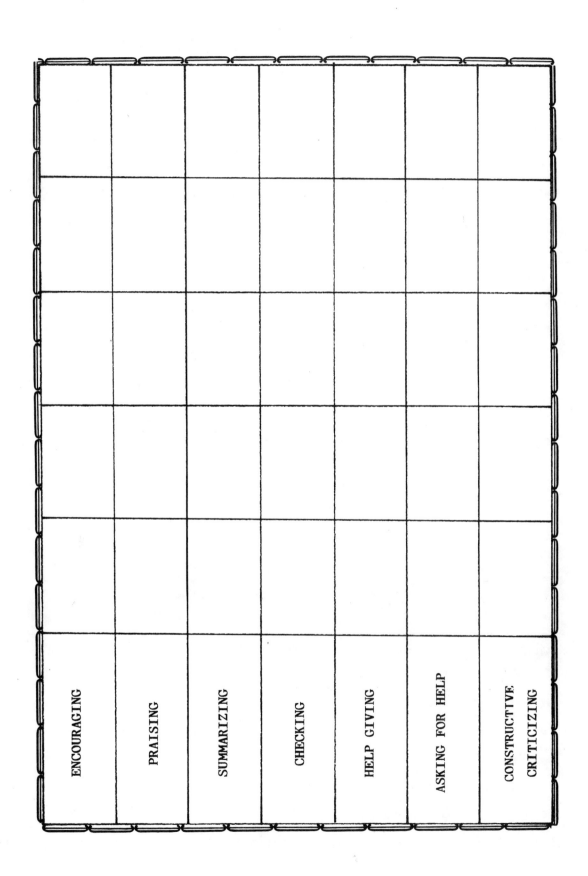

	ENCOURAGING	PRAISING	SUMMARIZING	CHECKING	HELP GIVING	ASKING FOR HELP	CONSTRUCTIVE CRITICIZING

☯ STUDENT CHECKLIST: Cooperation ☯

I contributed my ideas and information.

├────────────────────────────┼────────────────────────────┤
Always   Sometimes   Never

I asked others for their ideas and information.

├────────────────────────────┼────────────────────────────┤
Always   Sometimes   Never

I summarized all our ideas and information.

├────────────────────────────┼────────────────────────────┤
Always   Sometimes   Never

I asked for help when I needed it.

├────────────────────────────┼────────────────────────────┤
Always   Sometimes   Never

I helped the other members of my group learn.

├────────────────────────────┼────────────────────────────┤
Always   Sometimes   Never

I made sure everyone in my group understood how to do
the school work we were studying.

├────────────────────────────┼────────────────────────────┤
Always   Sometimes   Never

I helped keep the group studying.

├────────────────────────────┼────────────────────────────┤
Always   Sometimes   Never

I included everyone in our work.

├────────────────────────────┼────────────────────────────┤
Always   Sometimes   Never

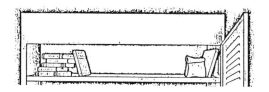

Cooperative Poetry: I, Too

EDYTHE JOHNSON HOLUBEC

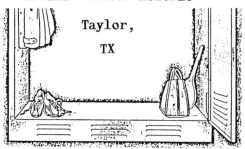

Taylor,
TX

Subject Area: English

Grade Level: Junior and Senior High

Lesson Summary: Students read a poem and answer questions about it.

**Instructional
   Objectives:**   Students gain practice in reading and understanding poetry, in sharing their interpretations of a poem, and in listening to and considering other interpretations and other points of view.

Materials:

ITEM	NUMBER NEEDED
Copy of **I, Too** (with discussion questions and agreement form)	One per student
Role cards	One set per group
Observation form	One per group

Time Required: One class period

≈ Decisions ≈

Group Size: Four (five if an observer is used)

**Assignment
to Groups:**   Teacher assigned, with a high, two medium, and a low
achieving student in each group.   Also, each group
should contain males and females and a mix of racial/
cultural backgrounds.

Roles: **Encourager:** Watches to make certain all group members
are contributing and invites silent members in by asking
them for their opinions or help.

Reader: Reads the poems to the group.   Also serves as
the **Praiser** who praises good ideas or helpful suggestions of group members.

Recorder: Records the group's answers and summarizes
each answer until the group is satisfied with it.

Checker: Checks to make certain group members can
explain each answer and the group's rationale for it.

Observer: (Optional) Does not take part in the discussion of the poem but observes the group's interactions,
records the behaviors on the Observation Sheet, and
reports to the group during the processing time.

≈ The Lesson ≈

Instructional Task:

*Your task will be to read a poem and answer the questions.   I want you
to come up with three possible answers for each question, then circle
your favorite.*

Positive Interdependence:

I want one set of answers from the group that you all agree upon.

Individual Accountability:

I will ask each of you sometime during the class period to give me the rationale for your group's answers.

Criteria for Success:

Your group will start with a grade of 100 on this assignment. I will pick someone at random to explain one of your group's answers to me. If s/he can do that, you will keep your score. If not, you will lose 10 points. I will check at least three of you on at least three of the questions.

Expected Behaviors:

I want to see each of you contributing and helping your group, listening to your group members with care, and pushing the group to look for all the possibilities before deciding on an answer. Also, your group will get a set of role cards. Pass them out randomly, read your role, and make certain you know how to do it before the Reader starts reading the poem. The Observer will report on how well s/he saw you performing your roles during the processing time. (If necessary, go over the roles to make certain the students understand them.)

❦ Monitoring and Processing ❧

Monitoring: Circulate among and listen to the groups. Check to make certain the groups are doing the task right (coming up with at least three possible answers, then agreeing on their favorite) and that group members are performing their roles.

Intervening: Feel free to interrupt while the groups are working.   Push groups to explore interesting answers and elaborate on superficial ones.   Praise examples of good group skills. If you see an interaction problem, encourage the group to stop and solve it before continuing.

Closing: After the groups have finished answering the questions, have a class discussion over the answers.   Pick group members at random to explain answers, keeping track of contributors and groups and grading groups accordingly.   List the groups' answers on the board, then see if the class can decide on answers all members agree on.

Processing: After the class discussion, have the groups get back together to process.   Have the observer report on what he/ she saw and show each group their marks on the observation sheet.   Then have the groups write down their answers to the following questions:

1.   *What behaviors did we do well?*
2.   *What behaviors do we need to improve upon?*
3.   *How well did we perform our roles?*
4.   *What would help us perform our roles better?*

If there is time, have the groups share some of their answers with the whole class.

◀ **Observation Sheet** ▶

	Group Members			
Contributes Ideas				
Encourages Others				
Praises Good Ideas				
Summarizes				
Pushes Deeper				

Other Helpful Behaviors Noticed:

I, TOO

by Langston Hughes

I, too, sing America.

I am the darker brother.
They send me to eat in the kitchen
When company comes,
But I laugh,
And eat well,
And grow strong.

Tomorrow,
I'll be at the table
When company comes.
Nobody'll dare
Say to me,
"Eat in the kitchen,"
Then.

Besides,
They'll see how beautiful I am
And be ashamed –

I, too, am America.

---

1. What are the emotions expressed by the poem?

2. What do you think/feel about what the poem says?

3. What are the three key words in the poem? (Be able to defend your choice.)

4. What is the poem saying?

To group members: *When you sign your name for the answers to these questions, it means that you have participated in the assignment and understand the questions and the answers. You also must agree with the answers and be able to explain them.*

The lesson developed around this poem was originated by Edythe Johnson Holubec, a high school English teacher in Taylor, Texas (and a sister to David and Roger).

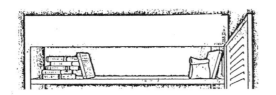

Computer Geography

TOM EGAN

St. Louis Park,
MN

Subject Area: Geography; Computer Skills

Grade Level: Junior High

Lesson Summary: Using a computer problem-solving simulation, students will work as a crew to sail an ancient ship to the New World and back in search for gold, using the sun, stars, ocean depth, climate, and trade winds to navigate.

Instructional Objectives: Students will learn higher-level problem-solving skills, and map-reading and navigational skills. They will improve their consensus-making and collaborating skills as well as their computer skills.

Materials:

ITEM	NUMBER NEEDED
Geography Search simulation game*	One per group
Computer	One per group
Daily worksheets	One per student
Final test	One per student
Role cards	One set per group
Navigational map	One per group

***Geography Search**, McGraw Hill, 1982.

 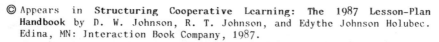

Time Required: Five instructional periods

≋ Decisions ≋

Group Size: Four

**Assignment
To Groups:**   Teacher assigned, with high, medium, and low achieving
students and males and females in each group.

Roles: **CAPTAIN:**

- **Task responsibilities** are to record
  ocean depth and the visual (what
  could be seen from the ship) report
  from the computer screen, and to
  make sure that no computer key is
  punched until the group comes to a
  consensus on its sailing decisions.
- **Maintenance responsibility** is to be a **Checker** who
  ensures that all group members understand and agree
  with the sailing decisions made.

NAVIGATOR:

- **Task responsibilities** are to record the information
  from the computer screen on the sun's shadow and the
  position of the stars and then to compute the ship's
  longitude and latitude.
- **Maintenance responsibility** is to be an **Encourager** who
  ensures that all group members share ideas and that
  no "put downs" occur.

METEOROLOGIST:

- **Task responsibilities** are to record from the computer
  screen the wind direction, speed, weather, and temperature, and to ensure that the correct wind direction is typed into the computer.

- **Maintenance responsibility** is to be a **Summarizer** who periodically summarizes the group's progress, decisions, and rationale for the decisions.

QUARTERMASTER:

- **Task responsibilities** are to record from the computer screen the provision report and to determine how many days of sailing are possible on the current provisions.
- **Maintenance responsibility** is to be a **Praiser** who compliments group members who do their assigned work and who contribute to the learning of their groupmates.

≈ The Lesson ≈

Instructional Task:

Your task is to work as a crew to sail an ancient ship to the New World and back in search for gold, using the sun, stars, ocean depth, climate, and trade winds to navigate. Initially, you will have to decide whether to go ashore, follow the coast, or sail your ship. The direction the ship can sail depends on the direction of the wind. Sailing, however, will cost your group in terms of supplies and hazards such as storms and pirates. So you must keep track of wind direction, wind speed, latitude and longitude, water depth, food provisions, temperature, and rain fall. Each day you should plan what to do, go to the computer and enter your decisions, record the results of your decision and any additional information the computer gives you, then leave the computer to plan your next series of actions. You need to plan carefully, because you might get blown back to shore, attacked by pirates, or may starve at sea.

Roles Assigned:

Your group will get four roles which you will randomly pick. You will rotate the roles so everyone will fill each role at least once. (Read and explain roles.)

Criteria for Success:

You will individually complete daily worksheets at the end of each period and take a final test on the last day over the material in the simulation. Your unit grade will be based on the average of your group's scores on the daily worksheets and the final exam. Also, you will be awarded bonus points on the basis of how much gold the total class accumulates -- ten percent of the gold all the cooperative groups accumulate.

Positive Interdependence:

For this assignment, I want you to work cooperatively. I expect you to perform your assigned role and to help each other master the material. Also, I will have the information you need to make effective decisions appear on the computer screen too briefly for any one student to copy all of it down, so you will need to be ready to perform your jobs. Remember that you get bonus points for how much gold the whole class accumulates, so help other groups when you can.

Individual Accountability:

You are responsible for performing your daily roles and for learning the material taught in the simulation so you can do well on the quizzes and test, and so you can help your group.

Expected Behaviors:

I expect to see everyone helping, everyone participating, and everyone performing his or her assigned roles. This means I will hear checking, encouraging, summarizing, and praising as I listen to your group working.

⤳ Monitoring and Processing ⤳

Monitoring: Monitor the groups closely to make sure that students fulfill both the task and maintenance aspects of their roles.

Intervening: If students become too involved with the computer, remind them to pay attention to the supplementary written materials.   Also, remind students of their roles, if necessary.

Processing: At the beginning of each day, students should check the scores of their group members on the quizzes and plan ways to raise their scores that day.   They should also evaluate how well they performed their roles yesterday and get hints for performing their new role from their group members. At the end of the unit, the class should evaluate how well they worked in their groups and how they could work together better next time.

AUTHOR'S NOTE

The oral interaction among students promotes considerable higher-level reasoning and learning.   Students learn leadership and social skills that are important for most careers.   I have often been surprised by the level of creativity generated by the cooperative interaction among students.   Using cooperative groups with computers is a natural partnership that enhances the effectiveness of both.

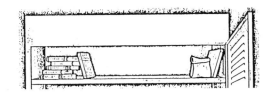

Identifying Skeletons

SUSAN WARD

Houston,
TX

Subject Area: Life Science

Grade Level: Junior High

Lesson Summary: Students are given pictures of skeletons of vertebrates and must figure out what they are.

Instructional Objectives: Students will gain practice in observing differences in various vertebrate skeletons, will identify animals by studying their skeletons, and will recognize adaptations of skeletons which enable the animal to survive in its environment.

Materials:

ITEM	NUMBER NEEDED
Pictures of 14 vertebrate skeletons Teacher transparency of the skeletons Answer key transparency	One per group

Time Required: Thirty to forty-five minutes

≈ Decisions ≈

Group Size: Three

**Assignment
To Groups:**   Either random -- by counting off, or teacher assigned with
high, medium, and low students in each group.

Roles: **Recorder:** Records the answers of the group.

Task-Master: Keeps the group on the task by watching the
time and not letting the group dwell on one skeleton too
long.

Encourager: Makes certain each member is
participating and invites any reluctant
members in by asking them for their ideas.

≈ The Lesson ≈

Instructional Task:

*Your group will be given a handout containing pictures of 14 modern-
day vertebrates' skeletons. You will have 15 minutes to identify the
14 animals by their skeletons.*

Positive Interdependence:

*I want one set of answers from the group. When you sign your name,
it means that you agree with the answers and can defend and explain
them. Also, you will each have a job to do to help the group achieve
the task.* (Explain the roles and randomly assign them.)

Individual Accountability:

*Each group member must be able to identify each skeleton and tell why
it fits that classification. I may ask any one of you to come to the*

overhead projector and point out the features of the skeleton that led to your group's identification of it.

Criteria for Success:

Groups that correctly identify ten skeletons will have mastered the task. Groups that correctly identify more than ten skeletons will receive bonus points.

Expected Behaviors:

I expect to see all group members participating, each one performing his or her role, and everyone justifying answers by pointing out features on the skeletons.

∽ Monitoring and Processing ∾

Monitoring: Circulate to see how the groups are doing and give hints when groups are at a standstill. Hints should be general, such as which class the animal belongs to (amphibian, reptile, etc.). Also, watch and encourage participation from all group members.

Closing: Identify the skeletons at the overhead projector and have the groups assess how well they did. Have members of groups that successfully identified the skeletons explain the answers to the groups that missed them.

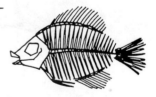

Processing: Comment on the behaviors you observed, then have each student tell their group members what they did best.

AUTHOR'S NOTE

The following skeletons can be included in the assignment: anteater, penguin, lion, hippopotamus, walrus, deer, kangaroo, frog or toad, camel, bat, crocodile or alligator, elephant, giraffe, and ape.

(This cooperative lesson is an adaptation of an activity by Kathy Kesting in **Science Scope**.)

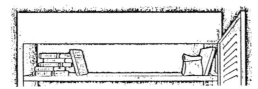

Geometry Polygons

CAROLYN BALDREE

Houston,

TX

Subject Area: Geometry

Grade Level: Junior or Senior High

Lesson Summary: Students learn to make polygons and triangles on geoboards.

Instructional Objectives:

1. Students will make regular polygons on the geoboards and then will create their own polygon design and name it.

2. Students will make different kinds of triangles on the geoboard and will be able to use the geoboard to answer specific questions about triangles.

Materials:

ITEM	NUMBER NEEDED
Geoboards	One per student
Rubber bands	
Triangle Worksheet	One per group

Time Required: Two class periods

≈ Decisions ≈

Group Size: Two

**Assignment
To Groups:**   Random. When students came to class, each received a card. On one set of cards were polygon **Shapes** and on the other set the polygon **Names**. Students found their partners by matching cards.

Roles: The student in the pair with the **Shape** was responsible for getting the needed supplies; the student with the **Word** was the answerer. Both were checkers for each other.

≈ The Lesson ≈

Instructional Task:

Lesson One: As a review the students were asked to make regular polygons--quadrilateral, pentagon, hexagon, heptagon, octogon, nonogon, and decagon--on the geoboard. When discussing quadrilaterals, the group made them on their geoboards with the **Shape** student doing the rectangle and the **Word** student doing the square. 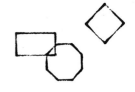 Then they made the parallelogram and the trapezoid. After comparing and contrasting both shapes, they were asked to make 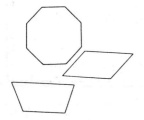 their own polygon design starting with a five-sided figure. Before one of the group could show his or her design to the class, both members had to figure out what it looked like and give it a name.   This procedure was done for polygons with six, seven, eight, nine, and ten sides. Then we had a contest to see which group could make a polygon with the most sides. Bonus points on the test were given to the winners. (This lesson could have been made into a **Charades** game with other groups trying to guess the names of each group's shapes.)

Lesson Two: As a review, the groups were asked to make triangles on the geoboards. The **Shapes** did triangles according to their sides and the **Words** did triangles according to their angles. Then they were asked the questions on the **Triangle Worksheet** about triangles and had to use the geoboard to prove their answers--verbal answers weren't accepted. (The teacher may choose to use all or part of the worksheet with each group.)

Positive Interdependence:

Even though each student had a geoboard, students needed each other in order to complete the task. In lesson one, students made their own polygon designs, but could not show them until their partners had agreed on a name. The group worked together on the polygon with the most sides. In lesson two, I told the **Shapes** to make triangles according to the sides and the **Words** to make triangles according to the angles. They checked each other's work and, if one was wrong, the other group member would explain it and then change it on the geoboard. For the questions, the students discussed and worked on the proofs together, then the **Word** students raised their hands to indicate that both were ready to show the proofs.

Individual Accountability:

In lesson one each student had to create a polygon design and name it. In lesson two, both made separate triangles and had to check each other in order to be successful. They did not know which of them would be asked to prove the answers.

Criteria for Evaluation:

In order to check all geoboards, I had students raise them in the air for each figure. This was a very effective way to see all geoboards. In lesson two, just being able to prove the answers with the geoboards instead of answering verbally was an evaluation in itself.

Expected Behaviors:

1. Stay with the group.
2. Use quiet voices when discussing and explaining to each other.
3. Both of you have to agree to the design's names in lesson one; in lesson two you have to agree upon the proofs before the Words can raise their hands.
4. Listen to your partner without interrupting.

≈ Monitoring and Processing ≈

Monitoring: Monitor to catch mistakes in the early stages and to help establish the rules for legitimate polygons. Also check to make certain students are following the expected behaviors.

Intervening: Intervene when you see a shape that is more than one closed polygon or when you see students with difficulties working together.

Processing: At the end of the lesson, have the groups write down two things they did well and the one thing they could improve. Discuss this orally after each lesson.

Ending: Briefly give an overview of the day's lesson, discussing definitions of polygons.

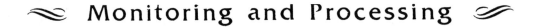

AUTHOR'S NOTE

In most typical
math classes the
lessons are taught in
such a way as to favor
the left-brain students. As
a result, these students are the
ones who "shine." In this lesson
the right-brain students were the
stars and they loved helping their left-
brain friends be a little more creative.
There was a new respect brought about for the
creative students from the other students.

Triangle Worksheet

1. Is it possible to make one triangle that is both acute and isosceles?

2. Is it possible to make one triangle that is both scalene and equilateral?

3. Is it possible to make a triangle that has two obtuse angles?

4. Is it possible to make a triangle that is both equilateral and obtuse?

5. Is it possible to make a right triangle that is isosceles?

6. Is it possible to make a right triangle that is equilateral?

7. Is it possible to make a triangle with two right angles?

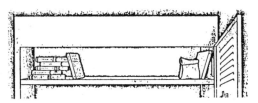

The Life and Works of Beethoven

LARRY STONE

Vineyard Haven,

MA

Subject Area: Music

Grade Level: Junior High

Lesson Summary: Students receive clues about the life of Beethoven which, if shared with their group, will help them answer questions about Beethoven.

Instructional Objectives: Students will learn specific facts about the life and works of Beethoven. They will also gain practice in using logic and in sequencing.

Materials:

ITEM	NUMBER NEEDED
Beethoven's Life Worksheet	One per student
Beethoven's Life Answer Key	One for teacher
Clue cards containing relevant and irrelevant facts about Beethoven	One set per group
Student Checklist	One per student

Time Required: One class period or less

≈ Decisions ≈

Group Size: Four

Assignment
To Groups: Teacher assigned, based on the teacher's prior knowledge
                of the students' varying levels. Make each group as heteo-
                geneous as possible.

Roles: None

≈ The Lesson ≈

Instructional Task:

Using the clue cards, students will read about the life and works of
Beethoven. The set of clues will be dealt out by
one member of each group until all the clues are
distributed.   No member may look at any clues
other than his own.   By asking each other questions about the clues, the students are to answer
the six questions concerning Beethoven's life.
Each student is to write the answers on h/her own
worksheet.   When every member of the group is

satisfied that their answers are correct, they should sign their names
to all of their group's answer sheets.

Positive Interdependence:

Each student receives only part of the information needed to complete
the assignment.   Everyone in the group must agree on the answers
before the group is finished, and all group members will receive the
same grade, based on their answers.

Individual Accountability:

Everyone will write the answers on their own paper and must signify that they agree with their group's answers by signing each of their group member's answer sheets.

Criteria for Success:

There are a total of ten answers. Any group which correctly answers all questions or misses only one will be given an **A**, two wrong answers a **B**, three wrong answers will be a **C**, and four incorrect answers will be a **D**. More than four wrong answers will receive a failing grade.

Expected Behaviors:

Tell the students that each group member is to be allowed to have his or her say about the questions and each group is to help their members understand the material covered in the lesson.

≈ Monitoring and Processing ≈

Monitoring: Walk around and observe the cooperation of the members of each group. Take notes on how the students are working to use while processing.

Intervening: Intervene only if the procedure is not being followed.

Processing: Review the behaviors observed during the lesson. Use anecdotal notes to describe behaviors you saw which helped the groups work together effectively. To insure that groups do not become competitive, during this feedback use the phrases, *I saw a group (do)* . . ." or *One group member (did)* . . . Then, ask each student to complete the student checklist individually and sign the paper. Then ask each student to name a social skill which s/he performed effectively that day. Ask the group to name a social skill which they performed effectively during the activity.

*Reprinted from **Structuring Cooperative Learning: Lesson Plans for Teachers** edited by David W. Johnson and Roger T. Johnson. Edina, MN: Interaction Book Company, 1984.

BEETHOVEN DID NOT VISIT
THE UNITED STATES NOR
ITALY

IT IS FAIR TO SAY THAT BEETHOVEN
DID NOT VISIT THE COUNTRY HE WAS
BORN IN

ONE OF BEETHOVEN'S TEACHERS
WAS VERY INTERESTED IN
CHURCH MUSIC

ONE OF BEETHOVEN'S TEACHERS
WAS FROM AUSTRIA

MR. ZIMMERMAN WAS NOT
ONE OF BEETHOVEN'S TEACHERS

WOLFGANG'S BROTHER HELPED
BEETHOVEN STUDY THE VIOLIN

THE TOWN OF WAHRING

IS ABOUT 20 MILES WEST

OF BERLIN, GERMANY

JOHANNE NEVER MET BEETHOVEN

BEETHOVEN IS BURIED IN A
GERMAN TOWN WEST OF BERLIN

THE CITY OF BERLIN IS
150 MILES FROM THE
WESTERN BORDER OF
GERMANY

𝓛𝓑

BEETHOVEN WAS BORN
IN 1770

BEETHOVEN WROTE MORE THAN
SEVEN SYMPHONIES

HIS FATHER WAS ONE OF SEVEN
CHILDREN, TWO OF WHOM
WERE JOHANNE AND WOLFGANG!

M. PFEIFFER AND F. ZIMMERMAN WERE
BOTH FROM AUSTRIA

VAN DER EDER WAS A VERY
RICH PATRON OF CHURCH MUSIC

BEETHOVEN WAS 57
YEARS OLD WHEN HE
DIED

MOZART, A GREAT
COMPOSER, LIVED IN
GERMANY

CARL OLSEN WAS BORN IN FRANCE

BEETHOVEN WROTE
LESS THAN 15 SYMPHONIES

BEETHOVEN WROTE MORE
THAN TWO SYMPHONIES

BEETHOVEN VISITED CARL
OLSEN'S HOME COUNTRY

LONDON IS IN ENGLAND, WHERE
QUEEN ELIZABETH REIGNS

BEETHOVEN VISITED M. PFEIFFER'S
HOMETOWN AND SAW THE TOWER OF
LONDON

BEETHOVEN VISITED ONE OF THE
THREE EUROPEAN COUNTRIES
LISTED ON ONE CLUE CARD

TO GET THE NUMBER OF SYMPHONIES HE
WROTE, ADD THE NUMBER 7 TO THE
LEAST NUMBER OF SYMPHONIES
THAT BEETHOVEN MIGHT HAVE
WRITTEN ACCORDING TO
THE CUES

$$\begin{array}{r} 7 \\ +\ ? \\ \hline \end{array}$$

ONE OF BEETHOVEN'S TEACHERS
WAS FROM ENGLAND

BEETHOVEN WAS BORN
IN A EUROPEAN COUNTRY

THE UNITED STATES

GERMANY, ITALY, AND AUSTRIA
ARE ALL IN EUROPE

BEETHOVEN WAS NOT BORN
IN ITALY OR AUSTRIA

Name _____

BEETHOVEN'S LIFE

1. In what country was Beethoven born? _____

2. How many symphonies did Beethoven write? _____

3. In what year did he die? _____

4. What are the names of three of the teachers he had as a student?

   _____   _____

   _____

5. What are the names of three of the countries he visited during his life?

   _____   _____

   _____

6. In what town was Beethoven buried? _____

BEETHOVEN'S LIFE

1,	In what country was Beethoven born?	Germany
2.	How many symphonies did he write?	Nine
3.	In what year did Beethoven die?	1827
4.	What are the names of three of Beethoven's teachers?	His father, M. Pfeiffer, van de Eder
5.	What are the names of three countries that Beethoven visited during his lifetime?	England, France, Austria
6.	In what town was Beethoven buried?	Wahring

Name _____

STUDENT CHECKLIST

PLACE A CHECK BESIDE EACH SENTENCE YOU FEEL YOU FULFILLED.

_____   1.   I followed the directions given by the teacher.

_____   2.   I shared the contents of my clues with the other
                group members.

_____   3.   I helped other members in my group to understand and
                answer the questions.

_____   4.   I received help from other members of my group when
                I needed it.

_____   5.   I asked other members of my group about their
                clues.

_____   6.   I felt that the task was finished or accomplished
                satisfactorily.

_____   7.   I felt that everyone in my group helped solve the
                answers to the questions.

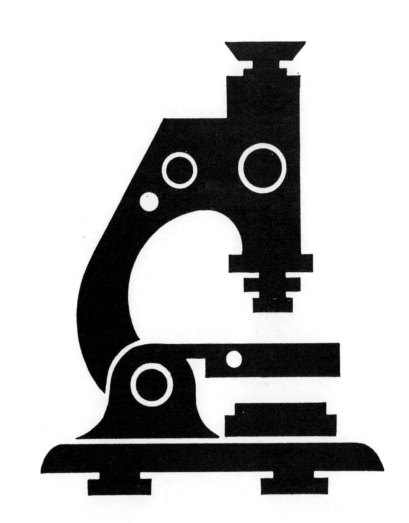

Senior High

A Valediction: Encouraging Cooperation

TOM MORTON

Vancouver,
British Columbia

Subject Area:	English
Grade Level:	Secondary
Lesson Summary:	Groups must match paraphrases with stanzas of John Donne's **A Valedication: Forbidding Mourning** and learn the target vocabulary. They then brainstorm comparisons with which they write a group poem containing metaphors.
Instructional Objectives:	Students will gain practice in reading and interpreting poetry, will develop an awareness of metaphor, and will learn to write metaphors.

Materials:

ITEM	NUMBER NEEDED
A Valediction: Forbidding Mourning by John Donne	One per student
Set of role cards	One per group
Set of task cards	One per group
Instructions/Evaluation sheet	One per group

Time Required: One and one-half hours

≈ Decisions ≈

Group Size: Three (four, if an observer is used)

**Assignment
To Groups:**   Either random or teacher assigned, with high, medium, and low achieving students in each group.

Roles: Reader of instructions/Checker of members to make certain they understand their roles, the instructions and the work

        Recorder of answers/**Encourager** of participation

        Reporter to the class/**Praiser** of contributions and efforts to practice the roles

        Observer of group interactions (optional)

≈ The Lesson: Part One ≈

Instructional Task:

Discuss some of the background of John Donne and **A Valediction: Forbidding Mourning.** Born in 1572, Donne was a contemporary of Shakespeare. Passionate, charming, and intellectual, Donne sailed with Sir Walter Raleigh on a raid against the Spanish Azores and wrote love poetry. He fell out of favor with the ruling class for secretly marrying his noble patron's sixteen-year-old niece. Although his marriage turned out to be a happy one, Donne was imprisoned for a time, lost his job, and lived in poverty for many years. In 1615 he became an Anglican minister and rose to prominence with his dramatic sermons and religious poetry as passionate as his earlier love poems. Donne wrote **A Valediction** to his wife before he visited the Continent in 1612. Donne had had a premonition of misfortune and on his return he found that his wife had given birth to a still-born child.

Distribute a copy of **A Valediction** and read it to the class. Explain that, in order to understand the poem fully, each group will be given a set of cards on each of which is a paraphrase of one of the stanzas of the poem. However, the cards are in a mixed order, so the group will have to sort them out, while following the instruction sheet carefully.

Positive Interdependence:

Students are all to agree on the answers of the group (consensus). Give the groups the role cards. Once each member has chosen and understood one of these roles, give the groups a set of task cards and an instruction sheet.

Individual Accountability:

Each member is to be ready to defend and explain the answers of the group. Their signatures at the end mean that they agree with the answer and can explain both it and the vocabulary.

❧ Monitoring and Processing ❧
Part One

Monitoring: First monitor the groups to check whether students can explain their group's decisions and the meaning of the vocabulary. Monitor the groups again to note the use of group skills.

Intervening: Comment on and praise those using the social skills. If there is a good opportunity to use a skill but a student does not do so -- for example, a worthwhile contribution that the praiser does not refer to -- encourage the use of that skill.   Intervene as well to ask individuals to explain the group answers.

Processing: Once students have completed the task and signed their paper, ask them to discuss and write group answers to the processing questions at the bottom of the sheet.

Closing: Have students hand in their answers and processing, then discuss the poem as a class.   At this stage you may wish to use a large compass to explain in detail Donne's extended metaphor in the last three stanzas or ask students for the explanation.

∾ The Lesson: Part Two ∾

Instructional Task:

For the following lesson, the ideas for teaching poetry from Kenneth Koch (**Rose, Where Did You Get That Red?**, Vintage, 1973, pp. 80-82) are combined with group brainstorming.   Koch says that **A Valediction: Forbidding Mourning** offers [children] new things to write about [science and math], and shows them how they can use these things to talk about tender and passionate feelings. . .by means of mechanical, mathematical, and scientific analogies.

First, you need to be sure that students are familiar with **brainstorming:** The purpose is to generate as many ideas as possible; there is no criticism or discussion of ideas until afterwards; group members try to build on others' ideas if they can, and do not worry too much about the "right" response -- they just want to get the ideas flowing. Later, the group reviews the ideas and chooses the best.   If the class is not familiar with brainstorming, teach and practice the process first.

Johnson, Johnson and Holubec

The group's learning task is to use brainstorming to make a list of at least twelve comparisons of a serious feeling like love or loneliness to things in science or math. From this list the group will choose the most interesting or exciting ones to develop into a group poem of at least six lines. The poem may have a comparison in each line or the group may devote the whole poem to one or two comparisons as Donne did with the compass metaphor.

Koch gives a number of examples and questions to help a class start: What feeling do I have that is like magnetism? Electricity? Human feelings and relationships can be compared to ordinary mechanical things like turning on a light switch, a bulb burning out, or an electric eye. Brainstorming an example as a class creates the enthusiasm for groups to launch into their own idea generation.

Positive Interdependence:

The group is to complete one list from which it makes one poem.

Individual Accountability:

Individual responsibility is harder with brainstorming which depends on the free play of ideas back and forth, so the teacher should reiterate the group roles as one way to ensure that everyone contributes: The **recorder** writes down the brainstorming and the poem as well as encourages participation; the **checker** sees that everyone understands what to do and proofreads the final product; and the **praiser** gives verbal support and also reads the completed poem to the class.

Criteria for Success:

Evaluation will depend on the teacher's purpose and the level of the class. Completion of the minimum number of ideas and lines and the use of correct English would be part of the criteria. Originality and vividness of the metaphor could also be evaluated in a more advanced class.

Expected Behaviors:

Tell students that you expect everyone to participate in the brainstorming and to perform their roles.

∼ Monitoring and Processing ∽

Part Two

Monitoring and Intervening: The teacher monitors as before for the use of social skills but, depending on the class experience, there may need to be additional intervening to help students brainstorm.

Closing: Have each group's reporter read its poem to the class.

Processing: Because group members have so recently discussed their use of collaborative skills and given a suggestion on improving their group process, their processing could start there:

1. What was your suggestion for improvement from the last class? Did you improve on that skill?
2. What were two other things that your group did well that helped you to work together?
3. How effective was brainstorming for generating ideas?

Then, as a whole class, ask for responses from several groups for a discussion of group process, especially on the social skills with which students may have trouble and on the brainstorming. You could also refer to the written responses from the previous exercise.

Exercise on:
A VALEDICTION: FORBIDDING MOURNING

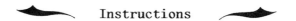 Instructions

Deal out the cards equally to each group member. Do not show your cards to other group members. On each card is a number and one or two sentences that paraphrase one of the stanzas of **A Valediction: Forbidding Mourning.** However, they are not in the correct numbered order. Your group task is to understand the poem by putting the paraphrases in the order that reflects the sequence of stanzas in the poem and also by finding out the meaning of the vocabulary used.

You need to share what is written on your cards, but must do so orally and not show or give your cards to anyone. You are to reach group consensus on the order of the numbers with each member able to explain why the group chose that order and able to give the meaning of any word.

Following are some particular words that, either by referring to the dictionary or using the context, you should be ready to define: **valediction, profanation, laity, trepidation, sublunary, breach, hearkens, obliquely.**

After reaching consensus, you have agreed that the numbered order of the cards should be: _____, _____, _____, _____, _____, _____, _____, _____, _____.

Signatures: Your signature means you have participated in the assignment and understand the poem. You also agree with your answers and are able to explain them and the meaning of the poem's vocabulary.

_____   _____

_____   _____

 Evaluation of Group Work

Discuss as a group and write down the answers to the following:
- Which of the cooperative skills did your group use successfully?
- What other things did your group do well?
- Which skills (if any) were harder to use?
- What one skill should your group try to improve next time?

A VALEDICTORY: FORBIDDING MOURNING
by John Donne

As virtuous men pass mildly away,
    And whisper to their souls to go,
Whilst some of their sad friends so say,
    "The breath goes now," and some say, "No,"

So let us melt, and make no noise,
    No tear-floods, nor sigh-tempests move;
'Twere profanation of our joys
    To tell the laity our love.

Moving of the earth brings harms and fears,
    Men reckon what it did and meant;
But trepidation of the spheres,
    Though greater far, is innocent.

Dull sublunary lovers' love
    (Whose soul is sense) cannot admit
Absence, because it doth remove
    Those things which elemented it.

But we, by a love so much refined
    That our selves know not what it is,
Inter-assured of the mind,
    Care less, eyes, lips, and hands to miss.

Our two souls therefore, which are one,
    Though I must go, endure not yet
A breach, but an expansion.
    Like gold to airy thinness beat.

If they be two, they are two so
    As stiff twin compasses are two:
Thy soul, the fixed foot, makes no show
    To move, but doth, if the other do;

And though it in the center sit,
    Yet when the other far doth roam,
It leans, and hearkens after it,
    And grows erect, as that comes home.

Such wilt thou be to me, who must,
    Like the other foot, obliquely run;
Thy firmness makes my circle just,
    And makes me end where I begun.

Task Cards

1

Yet our love, so special that we do not understand it, is strong in our minds and does not need us to be together physically.

2

People fear and puzzle over earthquakes, but they do not even notice the wobbling of the earth on its axis.

3

When good men die quietly and say their last words, their friends are not even sure that they are dead.

4

And so we will be the same: Like the outside foot of a compass, I must move away, but your steadiness will make me return home, just as the compass completes the circle.

5

Let us too be quiet and not cry aloud. To do so would be an insult to our great happiness.

6

Everyday physical love cannot last if the lovers are separated, because the source of their love is removed.

7

The two of us are united spiritually. Though I must leave, the separation will not break us apart, but only stretch our union.

8

Though your compass foot is fixed in the centre, when mine moves away, you lean towards my foot and then straighten up as mine returns to you.

9

We are like the two feet of a compass used for drawing a circle. You are the foot in the circle's centre that turns only if the outside foot does.

Great Greek Philosophers

ED HARRIS

St. Louis,
MO

Subject Area: World Studies, English, Social Studies

Grade Level: Secondary

Lesson Summary: Students learn the philosophies of Plato, Socrates, and
                           Aristotle, then decide what those philosophers' atti-
                           tudes would be toward current controversial topics such
                           as capital punishment, voluntary abortion, or South
                           Africa sanctions. They write a paper explaining their
                           conclusions and make an oral report to the class.

**Instructional
  Objectives:**   Students will learn the philosophies of three Greek
                           philosophers and will infer the philosophers' attitudes
                           toward current events.

Materials:

ITEM	NUMBER NEEDED
Observation sheet Library time and resources for class investigation	One per group

Time Required: Three to five days

≈ Decisions ≈

Group Size: Three

**Assignment
To Groups:**   Random; have students count off.

Roles: **Recorder:** Keeps tally points

Presenter: In charge of oral presentation

Proofer: Makes certain group members proofread each
other's written assignment

≈ The Lesson ≈

Instructional Task:

Assign each group member one of these philosophers: **Plato**, **Socrates**,
or **Aristotle**.   Students research the attitude of their philosopher in
the library and make a list of ideas embraced by him.

PLATO   **SOCRATES**   **ARISTOTLE**

Have students who studied the same philosopher meet together to share
ideas and brainstorm on the philosopher's attitudes.   This can be in
group size two to ten, depending on how you want to structure it.   The
objective is for students to help each other become experts on their
philosopher and to get each other ready for teaching the "home" groups
about their person.

Have students return to their groups of three and teach the other members about their philosopher.

Have groups select one of these controversial topics: **capital punishment, voluntary abortion,** or **sanctions against South Africa.** They then decide which philosopher would be for or against the issue, and they list at least five reasons why they think he would take that stand.

Have groups select the three best reasons and write a 1-2/3-2/3-2/3-4 power paragraph explaining why that philosopher would be for or against that issue.   Each member should produce a 2/3 and the whole group should collaborate on the 1 and 4.   (A 1-power sentence is a topic sentence, a 2-power sentence is a sentence stating a reason for power 1, a 3-power sentence is an example sentence of the power 2, and a 4-power sentence is a conclusion.)

Have each Recorder hand in a list of group members with the topic, pro or con, and philosopher.   Then have each Presenter present the group's arguments on the board.   Encourage class members to take issue at any time with the ideas of the presenter's group, but also encourage the presenter's group members to help defend the group's arguments.

Positive Interdependence:

Each group must research three philosophers, select one philosopher and match him with an issue, decide what that philosopher would think about that issue, write a report, make an oral presentation, and perform the roles.

Individual Accountability:

Each individual must investigate one philosopher and teach other group members about him, learn about the other philosophers, produce a portion of the paragraph, help prepare the oral presentation, perform roles, and model proper behavior.

Criteria for Success:

1. Ten points for the group's list of reasons on why the philosopher would be pro or con.
2. Forty points for the written paper.
3. Forty points for the oral presentation.
4. Two points for individuals who challenge presenting group's ideas.
5. One point for each five tally marks the teacher made on the observation sheet while observing the group.

Expected Behaviors:

1. Work together.
2. Share information.
3. Discuss pros and cons.
4. Listen and explain.
5. Use 6-inch voices.
6. Compliment good behavior.

≈ Monitoring and Processing ≈

Monitoring: Formally observe each group for a similar period of time using the Observation Form, giving tally points for proper behavior modeling. Informally, make sure that everyone participates and that each group meets the deadline for turning assignments in.

Intervening: Intervene in the groups to point out good behavior models, to explain or clarify difficult concepts, and to answer questions raised by the group.

Processing: At the end of the lesson, have the students evaluate how well they did on the lesson and how well they worked as a group. Have them set one group goal they will work on in the future.

OBSERVATION SHEET

Group Members: _____

_____

Behaviors Observed:

Working Together: _____

Sharing Information: _____

Discussing Pros and Cons: _____

Listening and Explaining: _____

Using Quiet Voices: _____

Complimenting Good Behavior: _____

TOTAL TALLY MARKS: _____

Divide by 5:

TOTAL BEHAVIOR POINTS: _____

Control Theory
in the Cooperative English Class

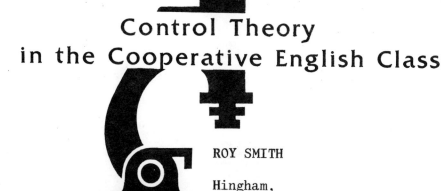

ROY SMITH

Hingham,
MA

Subject Area: English

Grade Level: Secondary

Lesson Summary: Students:

1. Prepare a list of basic human needs, how these needs affect their lives, and what behaviors help them fulfill these needs.

2. Read a story and complete a study guide helping them analyze how the main character behaves to meet his basic human needs.

3. Are tested on the story.

4. Apply what they have learned to their own lives.

5. Write an essay about the change in the way the main character attempts to meet his basic human needs; this essay is edited and proofread by fellow group members.

Academic
Instructional
Objectives: Students will:

1. Learn character analysis in the short story.

2. Learn control theory, the basis for Reality Therapy.

3. Improve their ability to write good essays.

Cooperative
Skills
Objectives: Students will learn and practice the task and main-
                 tenance skills of encouraging members to participate;

sharing information, ideas, and opinions; summarizing;
supporting and praising; giving feedback on spelling,
writing mechanics, grammar, and group participation; and
observing group interaction.

Materials:

ITEM	NUMBER NEEDED
A Summer's Reading by Bernard Malamud[1]	One per student
Student Study Guide	One per student
Test and Answer Sheet	One per student
Application Worksheet	One per student
Observation Sheet	One per group
Control Theory in the Classroom by William Glasser [2]	One per teacher

[1] Readily available since it is included in many anthologies
[2] Published in New York by Harper and Row, 1986

Time Required: Five class periods

≋ Decisions ≋

Group Size: Four. Students will have several different roles during
the unit. An observer will be used to record the interaction among the other three group members during one
part of this lesson.

Assignment
To Groups: To give students some power over class decisions and
still ensure a good mix, students select a partner to
work with and the teacher combines pairs into groups of

four to maximize heterogeneity.

≋ The Lesson ≋

Step 1: Brainstorming

State that during some parts of this unit students will be expected to focus on **quantity** of ideas and during other parts students will be expected to focus on **quality** of ideas. The purpose of the first activity is to brainstorm a list of as many different basic human needs (needs that underlie all human behavior) as the group members can think of. The basic rules of brainstorming are:

1. Record all ideas as to what the basic human needs are. The quantity of ideas counts, not the quality. Do not censor yourself.

2. All criticism or evaluation of ideas is forbidden. Do not try to decide if the ideas are good or bad, write every idea down.

3. All members should contribute ideas.

First, each student individually lists as many ideas as he or she can. Then students are assigned to cooperative groups of four. Group members are given the assignment of developing a group list by sharing their ideas with each other and generating as many additional ideas  as they can. During each cooperative assignment, students are expected to contribute their ideas, encourage everyone to participate, to praise others for their contributions, summarize information, and perform their assigned roles. Each group then reports to the entire class while the teacher writes a complete list on the board. The teacher should ensure that Glasser's basic needs are on the class list. Glasser's needs are:

1. The need to survive and reproduce so that our species will continue.

2. The need to belong (to love, share, and cooperate) by being

involved in relationships with others who care about one and are willing to provide assistance when it is needed.

3. The need for power to control oneself and to influence the people one is involved with.

4. The need for freedom to pursue the fulfillment of one's needs.

5. The need for fun, laughter, and enjoyment of life.

Step 2: Whole-Class Discussion

Hold a whole-class discussion to prepare a list of (1) how the basic needs affect their lives and (2) what behaviors help students fulfill their basic needs. Make sure the discussion focuses on Glasser's list of basic needs. Remind students that their behaviors are all they have to satisfy their needs. Whenever there is a difference between what they want and what they have, they must behave. To gain effective control over their lives, and to live responsibly, people have to satisfy what they believe is basic to them and learn to respect and not frustrate others in fulfilling what is basic to them.

Step 3: Read the Story

Students read the story individually, working by themselves without interacting with their classmates.

Step 4: Discuss the Study Guide Questions

Students are to meet in their cooperative groups. Assign the roles of:

1. Recorder/Praiser records the best answers of the group and praises helpful students and good answers.

2. Encourager watches to make certain everyone is participating and invites reluctant members to add to or comment on the discussion.

3. Summarizer restates the main ideas of the discussion so that mem-

bers can reevaluate and extend their thinking.

4. Observer observes the interactions among group members in order to provide information about how well the group is functioning.

Review the roles to ensure that students understand their responsibilities. The purpose of the group discussion is to produce high quality answers to each question on the study guide so that group members agree on the evidence about George's character (i.e., what he says and what he does). Their answers will be used to write about George's character and the principles of Glasser's control theory. Group members are to discuss each question thoroughly and agree on the best answer to each question the group can think of. Each member must be able to explain the rationale behind each answer. When the groups finish the answers are to be explained to the observer to see if the observer has anything to add. The group is then to review the story together to prepare for the quiz, which each member will take individually. Finally, the group is to discuss how well they worked together using the data recorded by the observer.

Step 5: Application

The most important part of teaching control theory through literature is the application to students' lives. Each student is to complete the Application Sheet. Each group member explains their application sheet with the rest of the group. Group members are to ensure that each member understands how to apply Glasser's control theory to his or her life. Remind students that they fulfill their needs by engaging in appropriate be-havior. Within their groups have them discuss examples of what they want, what behaviors they are engaging in to get it, whether the behaviors are effective, and what they might do differently.

Step 6: Test on the Story

Students take the 20-item test individually, without interacting with their classmates. If all members of a cooperative group score 85 percent or better on the test (17 questions correct), then each member receives five bonus points.

Step 7: Analysis of George's Character

Each cooperative group is to write an analysis of George's character. There is to be one analysis from each group, everyone in the group must agree, and each must be able to explain it to the rest of the

class. Explain that many people in George's position probably would not be able to change without help from a friend, parent, or counselor. Talking with such a person might reveal to George that he was causing his own misery by making bad choices. Explain the components of behavior: thinking, feeling, doing, and physiology. Give examples to demonstrate how people have the best chance of changing their misery by focusing on the

"doing component. A good example for teenagers is the misery they feel when they like someone who does not like them. Their control is to change the "doing" component.

Step 8: Writing

Working individualistically, without interacting with their classmates, students are to write an essay on George's character change in **A Summer's Reading**. The essay should discuss George's growth from irresponsible to responsible as defined by the principles of control theory. Glasser emphasizes that an individual has to take responsibility for his or her behavior. People can think anything they want to, but they are responsible for what they put into practice. **Respon-**

sible behavior is behavior that fulfills one's needs without interfering with other people's efforts to fulfill their needs. The thesis
of the essay should be: In A Summer's Reading Bernard Malamud shows
that people fulfill their basic needs through responsible behavior.
Students should refer to the Study Guide for ideas to include in their
writing. The essay will be graded on its:

1. Unity (sticks to one topic)

2. Coherence (well-ordered)

3. Full development (provides important information to develop the
    main idea, quotes from the story, and gives a relevant interpreta-
    tion).

4. Mechanical correctness.

Step 9: Editing Groups

Members of each cooperative group are to read each other's essays to
ensure their quality. Assign the following roles for editing:

1. Spelling checker ensures that all spelling is correct.

2. Mechanics checker ensures that capitalization and punctuation are
    are correct.

3. Assignment checker ensures that the essay fulfills the assignment
    as given by the teacher, that is, that the essay is unified,
    coherent, and fully developed.

4. Grammar checker ensures that the grammar is correct.

When the four group members are convinced that a member's essay is as
good as it can be, the member recopies it and the group members proofread it for final corrections and then sign their names to show their
approval.

? ! ? ... ! ... ? ! ?

∽ Monitoring and Processing ∾

Monitoring: This unit is to be taught during the fall term so that the principles of control theory may be used to analyze other stories later in the year. A number of new cooperative skills are introduced and, therefore, it is important to monitor students' behavior closely. Observe to see how each member of a group is fulfilling his or her assigned role. Look for positive actions that may be pointed out as examples of good group behaviors.

Intervening: When group members have problems in working together you may wish to intervene to help them develop the necessary cooperative skills or solve the problem. If some problems are widespread, it may be helpful to teach the entire class the needed cooperative skills. When appropriate, turn questions back to the group to solve. Students who are unskilled at working with others frequently ask questions of the teacher. Ask the questioner if he or she has consulted with other group members. Tell students they have the resources to solve most of their own problems; the teacher is a resource of last resort.

Processing: The observer collects data on the interactions of group members during Step 4. An observation form to help them do so is attached. The group then discusses and writes down (quality answers!) three things they did well in working together and one thing they are going to add to be even more effective next time. Remind students of these behaviors when they go into the next group session. Afterwards have students evaluate their progress and set a new goal for more effective behavior.

Evaluating: Give the students feedback on their test performance and on the quality of their essays. Read a particularly good essay to them. Discuss as a class what helped their groups do well.

A Summer's Reading

SUMMARY

In **A Summer's Reading** the main character, George, who is 20 years old when the story opens, quit school when he was 16, never returned and never attended night school, and has not been able to keep a job. Moreover, he spends most of his time alone, doing very little to find a job. He says during the story that one of the things he wants is for people to respect him, yet everything he does prevents him from gaining the respect he needs and wants.

The author contrasts George with an old man who is intelligent but whose life has been wasted. The suggestion is that if George continues on his current path he will end up like Mr. Cattanzara, who works in a change booth of a subway station. During the story, George meets Mr. Cattanzara several times and each time he lies to him about his summer reading. The lie makes George feel worse about himself and causes him to withdraw even more.

In his last meeting with George, Mr. Cattanzara who is drunk tells him, "George, don't do what I did." Some weeks later George hits a low point and rushes out to the library, sits down, and begins to read. The inference here is that George will now embark on a course of action that will allow him to feel better about himself and gain respect.

A Summer's Reading

STUDY GUIDE

As you read the story, answer the questions about the main character, George. Keep in mind the following definition: Responsible behavior is behavior which enables a person to fulfill his basic needs without interfering with other people's basic needs.

A. FAMILY SYSTEM

List the members of George's family and what you learn about each.

1. _____
2. _____
3. _____
4. _____

B. BASIC NEEDS

List George's goals or what he says he wants.

1. _____
   _____
2. _____
   _____
3. _____
   _____

C. IRRESPONSIBLE BEHAVIOR

List George's behaviors that make it impossible for him to get what he wants.

1. _____
2. _____

STUDY GUIDE (2)

D. SUPPORTING EVIDENCE

George lies during the story on at least five different occasions.
Identify each lie.
Explain his reason each time he lies.
Explain what he might do instead of telling a lie.

1. _____
    _____
2. _____
    _____
3. _____
    _____
4. _____
    _____
5. _____
    _____

E. COMPARISON OF CHARACTERS

List on the following chart the similarities and differences.

	GEORGE	MR. CATTANZARA
EXAMPLES	Young No job	Old Works in change booth

STUDY GUIDE (3)

F. INFLUENCE

There are three significant meetings in the story where George meets Mr. Cattanzara. Identify each. Describe what takes place. Explain how each meeting changes George.

1. _____
_____
_____
_____
_____
_____

2. _____
_____
_____
_____
_____
_____

3. _____
_____
_____
_____
_____
_____

G. RESPONSIBLE BEHAVIOR

Explain in what way George's behavior at the end of the story is considered responsible.

_____
_____
_____
_____

A Summer's Reading: Test

Select the one best answer from the four choices and place the number in the proper place on the answer sheet.

1. George

    1. likes to read books.
    2. likes people to think he reads books.
    3. likes people to think he is going to school.
    4. likes people to think he has a good job.

2. George is the product of

    1. a broken home.
    2. inferior schools.
    3. a poor environment.
    4. racial prejudice.

3. George believes

    1. reading is better than TV.
    2. reading is better than working.
    3. reading will bring him respect.
    4. reading will bring him a good job.

4. Which word <u>best</u> describes George's relationship with his sister?

    1. warm
    2. distant
    3. trusting
    4. fluctuating

5. Life is made bearable for George because

    1. his father and sister love him.
    2. he walks in the park.
    3. he keeps busy cleaning house.
    4. he is able to escape his problems by reading books.

6. The <u>best</u> word to describe George at the beginning of the story is:

    1. backward
    2. unmotivated
    3. carefree
    4. independent

Test (2)

7. George wanted to read books to

    1. impress others.
    2. learn about people.
    3. get back into school
    4. earn money from his sister.

8. Mr. Cattanzara seems to be

    1. confused about his own life.
    2. cheerful about his life.
    3. disappointed with his life.
    4. angry about his life.

9. Which word best describes George's feeling about himself?

    1. proud
    2. rebellious
    3. confused
    4. ashamed

10. George told Mr. Cattanzara that he was reading a hundred books on a list because

    1. he wanted to talk to someone about his reading.
    2. he wanted Mr. Cattanzara's approval.
    3. he wanted to borrow some books from Mr. Cattanzara.
    4. he wanted Mr. Cattanzara to see how smart he was.

11. People in this story think that others who read a lot are:

    1. sissies
    2. respectable
    3. wise
    4. thoughtful

12. In this story, the person most influential in George's life is

    1. Sophie, his sister.
    2. his father.
    3. the shoemaker.
    4. Mr. Cattanzara.

13. After a while, George tried to avoid Mr. Cattanzara because

    1. he was ashamed to face him.
    2. he had only read some of the books.
    3. he didn't want to be insulted any more.
    4. he couldn't remember what the books were about.

Test (3)

14. The best phrase to describe the way George sees Mr. Cattanzara is as

        1. an annoyance.
        2. his conscience.
        3. a competitor.
        4. a friend.

15. In this story George treats Mr. Cattanzara

        1. discourteously.
        2. sympathetically.
        3. affectionately.
        4. respectfully.

16. In his relationship with others, George is all of the following except

        1. a loner.
        2. a follower.
        3. a quitter.
        4. withdrawn.

17. Mr. Cattanzara offered George a nickel for lemon ice because

        1. George was a little boy.
        2. Mr. Cattanzara was drunk and made a mistake.
        3. George was acting like a little boy.
        4. Mr. Cattanzara liked to help people in need.

18. The word that best describes George at the end of the story is

        1. impatient.
        2. adventurous.
        3. restless.
        4. mature.

19. Near the end of the story after his confrontation with the drunken Mr. Cattanzara, George stayed in his room because

        1. he had a lot of reading to do.
        2. he was sick.
        3. he lost his self-respect.
        4. he was afraid the neighbors would make fun of him.

20. What does George want out of life?

        1. a job
        2. excitement
        3. respect
        4. to be left alone

A SUMMER'S READING
Answer Sheet

Name _____

1. _____	11. _____
2. _____	12. _____
3. _____	13. _____
4. _____	14. _____
5. _____	15. _____
6. _____	16. _____
7. _____	17. _____
8. _____	18. _____
9. _____	19. _____
10. _____	20. _____

A SUMMER'S READING
Answer Sheet

KEY

Name _____

1.	2	11.	2
2.	3	12.	4
3.	3	13.	1
4.	4	14.	2
5.	2	15.	4
6.	2	16.	2
7.	1	17.	3
8.	3	18.	4
9.	4	19.	3
10.	2	20.	3

APPLICATION

1. Write down what basic need you must fulfill
    in your life at this time.

    _____

2. What behaviors do you need to use
    to satisfy this basic need?

    _____
    _____
    _____

3. What are you doing now?

    _____
    _____
    _____

4. How is it helping?

    _____
    _____
    _____

5. What do you need to do differently
    to get what you need/want?

    _____
    _____
    _____

OBSERVATION SHEET

Contributing Ideas				
Summarizing				
Encouraging				
Praising				
Asking for Help				
Recording				

Cooperative Learning in the Library

CAROL GOLTZ

Anchorage, AK

Subject Area: Library Skills

Grade Level: Junior and Senior High

Lesson Summary: Students read an article of general interest and write a reaction to the article, generating questions they would like answered about the topic. Using a jigsaw format, they each study one source for finding material in the library, which they teach to their group members. They then obtain information from the library on the topic, using each of the resources studied. Students use this information to answer their previous questions.

Instructional Objectives: Students will gain a working knowledge of how to look up, locate, retrieve, and use magazine articles, newspaper articles, and books in the library.

Materials:

ITEM	NUMBER NEEDED
3 x 5 cards	One per student
Masking tape	Roll
An article of general interest	One per student
Reader's Guide Information Sheet	One per group
Newsbank Information Packet	One per group
Book Information Packet	One per group
Quiz (covering all three packets)	One per student

© Appears in Structuring Cooperative Learning: The 1987 Lesson-Plan Handbook by D. W. Johnson, R. T. Johnson, and E. J. Holubec. Edina, MN: Interaction Book Company, 1987.

Time Required: Four one-class periods

≈ Decisions ≈

Group Size: Three

Assignment
To Groups: Random, counting off to form groups of three.

Roles: None

Name Tags: Since, as Librarian, I don't know the names of the students in the classes I go into, I like to have a name tag
opening. Each student is asked to write his or her first
name on a 3 x 5 card, then four other items of information in the corners. I ask questions I think would be
fun as well as related to the kind of class and the topic
of research. One of my favorites is, "*If your class had
unlimited funds and powers to bring in any guest speaker,
living or dead, who would you want to come to your classroom?*" Share some of the responses. These name tags are
then taped to each student for the remainder of the
period. Frequently the classroom teacher thinks the
information in the corners would be interesting and/or
helpful, so collects the name tags at the end of the
period.

≈ The Lesson ≈

Instructional Task:

Day 1: *Read this article individually and write a reaction to it. In your reaction, be sure to list all the
questions you have about the subject. When they are fin-*

ished, list the questions as a class but do not answer them.

Day 2: *Number off to form groups of three. Your group will get three packets about using sources of information in the library. You are to each take one packet and study it individually. One of you will become the Readers' Guide to Periodical Literature expert, one will become the Newsbank expert, and one of you will become the Book expert. Learn your material well, because you will teach it to your group members, who need to know your material for a quiz and for looking up information in the library tomorrow.*

You have 10 minutes to study your material, 7 minutes to get together with someone studying the same material to share what you are going to teach and how you are going to teach it, 7 minutes apiece to teach your material to your group members, five minutes for an individual quiz over all three sections, and five minutes to discuss how well your triad functioned as a cooperative learning group. Give the packets to each group and let them decide who learns which.

Day 3: *Today for our topic, you are each to (1) obtain and photocopy a magazine article about it, (2) obtain and make a printout of a news-*

paper article on it, and (3) referring to the printout of the 57 bibliographic items on the WLN database, full out an interlibrary loan request for one of the books on that computer printout. By the end of the period, you must staple your three resources together and turn them in. However, no two students can submit the same articles or book request: You must check off a title once you have used it. (This takes some effort on the librarian's part to set out certain **Readers' Guides** and **Newsbank Indexes** for each group to use and a felt marker at the WLN printout so students can check off a title once they have used it. The effort pays off, however, since it prevents students from repeated: "It's checked out" responses from the library aides and "missing microfiche" experiences in the Newsbank drawers.)

Day 4: *Using the information you gathered yesterday, answer the questions we formulated on the article we read two days ago.* This can be done in the groups of three, or individually, with class discussion afterward.

Positive Interdependence:

. For the jigsaw, I want you to work cooperatively. That means that you are to learn all three sections and make sure that your group members have learned all three sections. You will receive points on how well your group members do on a quiz over all the packet material and on whether all three of you are able to find materials from all three sources in the library.

Individual Accountability:

You are responsible for learning your section of the jigsaw and teaching it to the members of your triad so that they (1) remember it for the quiz and (2) are able to find materials from your source when they go to the library. You are also responsible for learning all the information for the test and for finding materials from all three sources tomorrow in the library.

Criteria for Success:

You will get points which will add up to a grade on the following items: (1) participation, (2) the teaching notes on the cover of your packet, (3) the teaching notes of the group, (4) the points of your group members on the quiz over the packet material, and (5) whether everyone in your group finds three materials from all three sources.
(Teachers may want to vary the evaluation criteria.)

Expected Behaviors:

I expect to see everyone studying his/her packet, helping each other do a good job of teaching his/her material, listening carefully to each other, asking questions to make certain you understand, and reviewing for the quiz when the teaching is done.

≈ Monitoring and Processing ≈

Monitoring:
: The librarian and the teacher help the students do the task as they are working and keep them aware of time limits. They also watch for and record instances of helpful cooperative behaviors to tell about during whole-class processing.

Intervening:
: If any groups seem to be having trouble, the librarian or teacher may want to help group members define what the problem is and figure out a way to solve it. Often the students, with teacher guidance, can get themselves back on track.

Processing:
: It is crucial to allow a few minutes to process or share feelings about the cooperative learning experience. The groups should answer: (1) How did you feel when you were asked to become an expert? (2) How did you feel about being responsible for someone else's learning? (3) What behaviors in your group promoted learning? (4) What behaviors made you uncomfortable or angry? Share some of these comments with the whole class, along with your observations during monitoring to demonstrate that certain social skills really do foster learning, that they cannot be assumed, but must be taught and developed.

AUTHOR'S NOTE

Student rapport is crucial. High school students need to understand the rationale behind name tags, assigned groupings, and accountability before they're going to buy into a cooperative method. Also, rapport with the classroom teacher is crucial. Making certain he or she knows what you are going to do and why, planning together, and having set responsibilities during monitoring are helpful. This lesson is most successful when the adults and students involved have some background in cooperative learning strategies.

READERS' GUIDE TO PERIODICALS

Packet

Questions to answer before teaching your partners:

1. What type of material does it index?

2. Why are there so many different guides?

3. How do you select which guide to use?

4. How do you interpret a specific entry in the guide?

5. Where can you get help regarding the abbreviations used?

6. How do you know whether or not the library has a particular magazine?

7. How do you actually get the magazine article itself?

8. How far back does the library keep issues of magazines?

9. What magazines are available on microfiche and/or microfilm?

10. When are magazines a good source of information? When are magazines a poor place to look for information?

Attach xerox copies of these pages: Abbreviations of Periodicals Indexed, Abbreviations, a sample page from the Readers' Guide, a guide for translating entries, and a copy of the Magazine Request slip. Write on those pages any helpful comments or questions which can direct the students' reading and learning.

NEWSBANK MICROFICHE Packet

Questions to answer before teaching your partners:

1. What kind of information does it index?

2. Why are there so many different indexes?

3. How do you select which index to use?

4. How do you interpret a specific entry in the index?

5. Where can you get help regarding the abbreviations used?

6. How do you know whether or not the library has the actual microfiche referred to in the index?

7. Where do you get the actual microfiche card you want to use?

8. How do you read the information on the microfiche?

9. How do you get a printed copy of the information on micro-fiche?

10. When is **Newsbank** a good source of information? When is it a poor place to look for information?

Attach xerox copies of these pages: An introduction to NewsBank, Steps in Using NewsBank, New Index Terms for 1985, two pages from the **NewsBank** Index, and a **NewsBank** sample request slip. Write on those pages any helpful comments of questions which can direct the students' reading and learning.

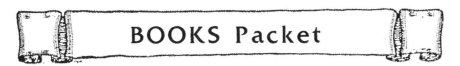

BOOKS Packet

Questions to answer before teaching your partners:

1. Where do you find the indexing for books in the library?

2. Why are certain books identified as "reference" books?

3. Where are the reference books shelved in this library and what common letter do they have in their call number?

4. How do you know whether or not the library has books on a specific subject?

5. If you can't find a book on a specific subject you look up, what could you try looking up next?

6. If this library doesn't have a particular book that you want, how can you find out if another school in the district has it, and, if they do, how can you get it?

7. Why is an index especially important in reference books?

8. When is it preferable to use a non-reference book rather than a reference book?

9. How do you actually check out books from the library and what restrictions are there on reference book checkout?

10. When are books a good source of information? When are books a poor place to look for information?

(Attach xerox copies of these pages: a page from **Books in Print**, a page of a computer printout of a **WLN** search, a page of a subject search on **WLN**, and a copy of an **Interlibrary Loan Request** form. Write on those pages any helpful comments or questions which can direct the students' reading and learning.)

Decision on Dieppe

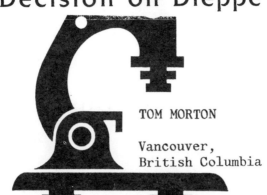

TOM MORTON

Vancouver,
British Columbia

Subject Area: Social Studies

Grade Level: Secondary

Lesson Summary: Pairs of students prepare positions either for or against the Dieppe Raid in World War II. In groups of four the pairs argue their positions, discuss and question each other, then change sides and argue for the opposition. The groups of four reach consensus, then write a paper delineating and supporting their conclusion.

Instructional Objectives: Students will learn about the Dieppe Raid as an important event in Canadian history at the same time as they get practice in clarifying or framing an issue, distinguishing fact from value, evaluating evidence, persuading, summarizing, and disagreeing constructively.

Materials:

ITEM	NUMBER NEEDED
Situation Sheet	One per group
Procedure and Rules Sheet	One per group
Raid on Dieppe: Pro	One per group
Raid on Dieppe: Con	One per group
Observation Sheet	Two per group

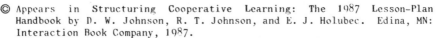

Time Required: Three one-hour class periods

≈ Decisions ≈

Group Size: Four

**Assignment
To Groups:**   Make random groups, by having students count off (a class of 28 would count off by seven to form groups of four), then assign students within each group to subgroups of two by pairing students whose names are first in the alphabet.

Roles: None

≈ The Lesson ≈

Instructional Task:

Early in the Second World War, after Germany had succeeded in conquering most of continental Europe, the Allied generals decided in the spring of 1942 to launch a large raid of about 5,500 troops, of whom  *5,000 were Canadian, to test the enemy defenses. The raid was planned for July 4th against the French port of Dieppe. Unfortunately, bad weather forced the cancellation of the raid. On July 15, 1942, the generals held a meeting to decide whether or not the raid would be conducted in early August. Your task will be to gather as much information as you can about this situation, argue both points of view in order to examine them carefully, reach consensus as to whether or not the raid should be conducted, and present a reasoned, factual, and persuasive ration as to why the decision is correct.*

The procedure is as follows: You will be working in groups of four. During the first class period, your group of four will subdivide into pairs. One pair will be **for** the raid, one pair will be **against** it. You will be given readings and information to support your pair's position. You will have time to read and discuss your material with your partner and plan how best to advocate your assigned position so that (a) you learn the information and perspective within the articles and technical reports, (b) the opposing team is convinced of the soundness of your team's position,

and (c) the members of the opposing team learn the material contained within your readings.

During the second class period, both teams will present their positions, and then engage in a general discussion in which they advocate their position, rebut the opposing position, and seek to persuade the opposing team to adopt their position and reasoning. You will need to take notes and clarify anything you don't fully understand when the opposing team presents and advocates its position.

On the third day, the teams will reverse positions and argue for the opposing side. Then you will drop your positions and, with the information and arguments you've accumulated, you will reach a consensus about the issue and prepare a group report detailing your group's decision and supporting it with information and rationale.

Positive Interdependence:

For this assignment, I want you to work cooperatively. Each pair is to present a joint presentation advocating its position. Each group is to reach consensus on whether the Dieppe Raid should or should not have been conducted and submit one written report detailing its conclusion and presenting a reasoned and convincing rationale as to why its decision is valid.

Individual Accountability:

You are responsible for helping your pair study and present its case and for helping the group reach consensus and write its position paper. I expect each of you to be prepared to be called on to present and support your group's decision orally in front of the class.

Criteria for Success:

The group report will be evaluated on the basis of the quality of the writing and on whether it contains a reasonable defense, supported by evidence, of the group's opinion.

Expected Behaviors:

I expect to see everyone following the rules for constructive criticism (go over handout), *particularly criticizing ideas, not people. I also expect to hear you paraphrasing and encouraging. I will be observing for these behaviors* (show students the Observation Form) *and will give you feedback on how well I see you do them.*

≈ Monitoring and Processing ✑

Monitoring: While the students are working, watch to see how well they are doing the task. Energize any lagging pairs and help keep the class aware of time limits. Use the Observation Sheet to formally observe the groups once every period, so the groups will have it to use when they process their group interactions.

Intervening: If any student does not seem involved, ask him/her to tell you the position being argued or discussed in the group at the moment. If students are not following the **Rules for Constructive Controversy**, point this out and ask them to adhere to the rules. Praise good examples of criticizing ideas, paraphrasing, and encouraging as you see them.

Processing: Either daily or at the end of the three-day activity, give
               the groups the observation sheets you filled out on them
               and ask them to write down at least two comments about what
               went well in their group and one comment on what their
               group could do better next time. These are to be handed
               in with the report and kept on file. Then conduct a class
               discussion on what helped the groups effectively fulfill
               their task.

✦ AUTHOR'S NOTE ✦

For my students -- and myself, too -- conflict is tough. It easily draws
lines, fences, then walls that opposing sides never cross. Or, it is
avoided altogether, sometimes in hushed, fearful tones. Yet my students
welcome conflict and, when class discussion veers to the controversial,
even cry out "debate, debate." Teaching my students effective controversy
skills raises interest and motivates them to probe deeper and seek more
information and opinion. It produces higher-level student learning and
promotes the development of social skills. One caution in using this
lesson, however: **Conflict resolution is a complex skill that builds on
collaborative skills the students should have already learned.**

Situation: Dieppe

Allied Headquarters, July 15, 1945

Since World War II began on September 3, 1939, Germany has succeeded in conquering most of continental Europe. It is opposed by the Allies: Great Britain, Canada, Russia, the United States and other countries. Great Britain is still free and its armies are fighting in North Africa. Much more severe fighting is on the Russian front, Germany having invaded Russia in 1941. To defeat Hitler's Germany, eventually the Allies must open a second front and invade the European continent from Great Britain. However, the Allies are not yet prepared, as only 12 divisions are stationed in Great Britain as compared to 26 German divisions ready to defend an invasion across the English Channel. More troops and supplies are only moving slowly to Great Britain from North America because of attacks by German submarines. However, to help gain knowledge and experience for a future invasion, the Allied generals decided in the spring on a large raid of about 5,500 troops, of whom 5,000 are Canadian, to test the enemy defences. The troops are well prepared.

The best tide, weather, dawn, and man conditions were during a few days in early July and mid-August, so a pre-dawn surprise attack was planned for July 4th against the French port of Dieppe. Unfortunately, bad weather forced the cancellation of the raid. A third of the soldiers went on leave.

It is now July 15, 1942, and a chance to reconsider. You are to take the part of a Canadian general meeting with British generals. Do you go ahead with a raid in August? You will, at the end, have to make a written report to British Prime Minister Winston Churchill.

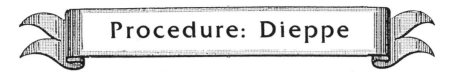

Procedure: Dieppe

1. Meet with your partner and plan how to argue effectively for your position. Make sure you and your partner have mastered as much of the material supporting your position as possible. You have 20 minutes for this.

2. Meet with another pair preparing the same position as you have. Exchange arguments and information and help prepare each other to argue effectively. You have 10 minutes for this.

3. Present your position to your group of four and listen to their position. Be forceful and persuasive in your presentation. Take notes and clarify anything you do not fully understand when the opposing pair presents its position. You have 5 minutes.

4. Open discussion. Argue forcefully and persuasively for your position, presenting as many facts as you can to support your point of view. Critically listen to the opposing pair's position, asking them for the facts that support their point of view. Remember, this is a complex issue and you need to know both sides to write a good report. Work together as a total group to get all the facts out. Make sure you understand the facts that support both points of view. You have 10 minutes.

5. Reverse positions. You must argue the other pair's position and they must argue yours. In arguing for the opposing pair's position, be as forceful and persuasive as you can. See if you can think of any new facts that the opposing pair did not think to present. Elaborate on their position. You have 10 minutes.

6. Seek consensus. Try to find a group decision that all four of you can agree with. Summarize the best arguments for both points of view. Detail what you know (facts) about World War II and Dieppe. When you have consensus in your group, organize your arguments to present to the entire class. Other groups may make the opposite decision and you may need to defend the validity of your decision to the entire class. You have 10 minutes for this.

7. Write your report. Remember that it will be graded on how well you support the decision you made and on how well-written it is. When you are certain your report is as good as you can make it, sign it. You have 30 minutes for this.

8. Process your group's interactions by answering the following questions: 1. How well did we do the behaviors observed for? 2. What are two behaviors that we did particularly well as a group? 3. What is one behavior we could do even better next time?

Rules for Constructive Criticism*

1. I am critical of ideas, not people. I challenge and refute the ideas of the opposing pair, but I do not indicate that I personally reject them.

2. I remember that we are all in this together, sink or swim. I focus on coming to the best decision possible, not on winning.

3. I encourage everyone to participate and to master all the relevant information.

4. I listen carefully to everyone's ideas, even if I don't agree.

5. I restate what others have said, especially if it is not clear.

6. I first bring out ALL the ideas and facts supporting both sides, and then I try to put them together in a way that makes sense.

7. I try to understand both sides of the issue.

8. I change my mind when the evidence clearly indicates that I should do so.

*Taken from: *Creative Conflict* by David W. Johnson and Roger T. Johnson. Edina, MN: *Interaction Book Company*, 1987.

Raid on Dieppe: Pro

The Proponent's Viewpoint

Your position is to launch the attach as planned on Dieppe in August. Whether or not you agree with this position, argue for it as strongly as you can. Take the proponent's viewpoint honestly, using arguments that make sense and are rational. Be creative and invent new supporting arguments. Seek out information that supports your position. If you do not know needed information, ask members of other groups who may know. Remember to learn the rationale of your position and those who oppose the August raid. Challenge the opponents' position; think of loopholes in their logic; demand facts and information to back up their arguments.

1. Our responsibility is to win the war for our country. If Europe is lost, Germany will then invade North America. Russia is an important ally that is now doing most of the fighting. It may be defeated or surrender. They are pressuring us to open a second front to divert German troops away from Russia. Allied public opinion and the U.S.

Government agree with the Russians. A large-scale raid will show both the Russians and Germans that we are serious about an invasion as soon as possible and will divert German troops as well.

2. For the future invasion, we need to gain experience and knowledge about amphibious landings in large numbers and the enemy defence systems. A large raid will give us this vital information.

3. It's far too late in the year to plan for another raid in force and the Canadian army is ready.

4. Troop morale is vital. The Canadians have been sitting in Britain since late 1939, spoiling for action. When the July raid was cancelled, there was great disappointment. Soldiers in a war are trained to fight and they must do so to keep spirits high.

5. Morale at home is vital. People must make sacrifices to produce the goods and materials we need to fight the war. Nothing raises morale at home like hearing of battles won and progress being made in victories to give hope and dedication.

6. A well-planned attack in the darkness before dawn, without advance warning by naval and aerial bombardment will catch the enemy surprised and unprepared.

 Raid on Dieppe: Con

The Opponent's Viewpoint

Your position is to oppose any attack on Dieppe. Whether or not you agree with this position, argue for it as strongly as you can. Take the opponent's viewpoint honestly, using arguments that make sense and are rational. Be creative and invent new supporting arguments. Seek out information that supports your position. If you do not know needed information, ask members of other groups who may know. Remember to learn the rationale of your position and those who oppose the August raid. Challenge the proponents' position; think of loopholes in their logic; demand facts and information to back up their arguments.

1. Our responsibility is to win the war for our country and to lose as few lives as possible. We cannot needlessly risk lives. Dieppe is very heavily defended. Our intelligence reveals gun batteries, anti-tank obstacles, barbed wire, and machine guns. Moreover, amphibious operations are very difficult. The last such attack, on Gallipoli in 1915, was a horrible disaster.

2. The Germans may well be prepared. A third of the men ready to go on the July raid have been on leave without restriction on talking about what they have been doing. German spies must have heard. Security is broken. The risk is too great that the Germans will be waiting, prepared. We cannot waste lives. It will lessen troop numbers and seriously hurt morale.

3. We all agree we are not yet ready for a full invasion. We need a year or two to build up enough troop and supply strength to succeed in an invasion. It's a waste to invade now.

4. There are other ways to gain information on enemy defences. A small commando raid of a few hundred would have more chance of surprise and less risk of loss of life.

5. We are already doing all we can to fight the war and aid our ally Russia. British, Canadian, and other troops are fighting in North Africa. United States and Canadian ships are trying, despite submarine attacks, to send supplies north of Scandinavia to Russia.

6. Any major attack needs strong artillery and air force bombardment first to weaken enemy defences. To attack without it means failure.

Observation Sheet for Conflict Resolution

	Group Members			
Criticizing ideas, not people				
Restating or paraphrasing				
Encouraging				
Additional skills:				

Comments

Choosing and Financing an Automobile and Computing Transportation Costs

LUCILLE GROULX

Kalamazoo,
MI

Subject Area: Consumer Math

Grade Level: Secondary

Lesson Summary: Using information sheets about the costs of buying and running an automobile, student must agree on the most economical car to buy for a family of four and must work math problems based on their decision.

**Instructional
  Objectives:**   Students will gain practice in decision making and mathematical computation, and will build their awareness of automobile fuel conservation.

Materials:

ITEM	NUMBER NEEDED
Transportation Fact Sheets I & II	One per student
Average Driving Statistics	One per student
Situation and Decisions Worksheet	One per group
Math Problems Worksheet	One per student
Observation Sheet	One per group

Time Required: Three to four class periods

∽ Decisions ∾

Group Size: Four

Assignment
To Groups: Random, by counting off, or teacher assigned to ensure that
              heterogeneous racial, sex, and math competency factors
              exist in each group.

Roles: Checker: Makes sure everyone has completed his/her share
              of the math problems, and that all group members know how
              to do each of the math problems.

              Recorder: Reads the situation narrative to the group,
              records the group's decisions on the Decision Worksheet,
              and records the group's math computations on one Math Work-
              sheet to be submitted to the teacher.

              Questioner: The only person in the group who is to direct
              group questions regarding the assignment to the teacher.
              This person will return to the group and inform members.

              Observer: Records the actions of each group member on an
              observation sheet; does not participate in the group while
              observing.

∽ The Lesson ∾

Instructional Task:

When the groups are in place, distribute the materials and randomly
assign the roles. Explain that each group is to hand in one Decisions
Worksheet, one Math Worksheet, and one Observer Sheet. Clearly state
that all computation work must be shown. Motivate the students to
consider fuel and money conservation by offering a prize to the group
that succeeds in saving the most money under the budgeted transportation amount.

Positive Interdependence:

Explain that you want one paper from the group that all members agree on and on which they can explain the answers. Remind them that everyone is to cooperate in the decisions involving a car choice, size, number of cylinders, type of transmission, and the length of financing. No one is finished until all members of the group are finished.

Individual Accountability:

Make certain that students understand that you expect them to divide the math problems among group members, with each teaching the other group members how to complete the problems.

Criteria for Success:

Groups will get ten points for each math problem, and they will receive one group grade.

Expected Behaviors:

Tell students that you expect them to work together and to help each other understand how to do the math involved.

~ Monitoring and Processing ~

Monitoring: While the students are working, move from group to group to observe the degree of cooperation occurring and to assist students in needed math skills. Respond to **Questioners** from groups and observe how the **Questioners** share the information upon their return to the groups.

Intervening: Reteach math skills as needed. Also, point out problems in the social skills of the groups and help the groups resolve the problems.

Processing: Each day, have the **Observer** report to the group the inter-
               action patterns observed and have the groups decide what
               they do well as a group and what they need to improve upon.

Ending: Have the group teach the **Observer** how to complete the math
               problems. Then score the math worksheets and inform the
               groups of the grade they received.

Reprinted from **Structuring Cooperative Learning: Lesson Plans for
Teachers** by Roger T. Johnson and David W. Johnson (Eds.). Edina:
Interaction Book Company, 1984.

⊚ SITUATION ⊚

A family of four (two parents and two children--ages 8 and 10) need to buy an automobile. They have $4,000 in a savings account from which they can withdraw 1/4 of the price of an automobile to cover the down payment. They also have a yearly budgeted amount of $3,540 which must cover their transportation costs.

Your goal is to spend less than this budgeted amount ($3,540) for the year on transportation costs. The group that saves the most money to be deposited in the family's savings account will win the prize.

You are to discuss the decisions below that must be made and come to agreements with at least three other people. You are also to work the math problems dealing with transportation costs cooperatively, and share the information with each other. Only one decision paper and one math worksheet is to be turned in for each four people. All four persons are to sign the decision sheet and the math problem worksheet to show that you agree as to the decisions and answers, and that you all understand how to work the problems.

⇥ DECISIONS ⇤

Date _____   Group Number _____

1. The automobile of our choice is _____ (make of car).

2. It is a minicompact ____; subcompact ____; compact ____; mid-size ____;

   large/full-size ____. (Check one)   Number of cylinders _____

3. This automobile has an automatic ____; manual ____ transmission.

   (Check one)

4. The total price of this car is _____.

5. Its estimated gas mileage for urban (city) driving is _____.

   (Deduct *five* miles from the highest estimated mileage.)

6. The length of financing is for one ____; two ____; three ____ years.
   (Check one)

Signatures

_____   _____   _____

Transportation Fact Sheet I

MINICOMPACTS

Datsun 210	$5,000	Dodge Colt	$5,000	Pinto	$3,900
		Ford Mustang	$5,100		

Approximate weight: 1900 lbs.

SUBCOMPACTS

AMC Gremlin	$5,000	Buick Skyhawk	$5,211	Chevette	$5,000
Datsun 510	$5,700	Datsun 810	$8,300	Ford Fiesta	$5,000
Audi Fox	$5,000	Toyota Celica	$6,400	Pontiac	
Rabbit	$6,000	Mazda Wagon	$4,170	Firebird	$5,000

Approximate weight: 2800 lbs.

COMPACTS

AMC Concord and Pacer	$6,000	Buick Skylark	$5,340		
Chevrolet Nova	$5,300	Dodge Aspen	$5,000	Ford Grenada	$5,200

Approximate weight: 3400 lbs.

MID-SIZE

Buick Century	$7,000	Regal	$ 6,505
Chrysler Cordoba	$6,500	Cadillac Eldorado	$14,500
Pontiac Grand Prix	$7,000	Ford Fairmont	$ 5,500

Approximate weight: 3700 lbs.

LARGE/FULL-SIZE

Buick Electra	$9,424	LeSabre	$6,844
Olds Delta	$6,800	Buick Riviera	10,371

Approximate weight: 4800 lbs.

Johnson, Johnson and Holubec

Transportation Fact Sheet II

Vehicle Selection: Automobile Mileage Guide

Size					
Minicompact	4	Manual	20–36	31–48	23–40
Minicompact	4	Automatic	23–29	28–38	25–32
Subcompact	4	Manual	17–35	25–46	20–39
Subcompact	4	Automatic	17–30	20–36	18–33
Subcompact	6	Manual	14–20	23–28	17–23
Compact	6	Manual	18–20	25–28	19–23
Subcompact	6	Automatic	14–20	21–27	17–22
Mid-size	6	Manual	16–21	25–33	14–24
Compact	6	Automatic	16–20	21–27	18–23
Compact	8	Manual	15–16	21–25	17–19
Mid-Size	6	Automatic	17–19	22–27	19–22
Compact	8	Automatic	10–16	17–22	13–19
Mid-size	8	Manual	15–20	22–29	18–23
Mid-size	8	Automatic	10–19	14–27	11–22
Full	8	Automatic	10–18	15–25	11–21
Sports cars/ two seaters	8	Manual	14–16	19–26	16–19
Van	6	Manual	17–18	24	20
Van	6	Automatic	16	22	18–19
Van	8	Manual	14–15	18–22	15–17
Van	8	Automatic	12–15	17–19	14–16

Average Driving Statistics

♣ The average driver travels 15,000 miles per year.

♣ The average driver spends $1.20 for a gallon of gas.

♣ Car insurance costs approximately $350.00 per year.

♣ There will be five oil changes over the year
    amounting in cost to $75.00.

Math Problems Worksheet

All work must be shown.

1. The down payment for your automobile choice is $\frac{1}{4}$ the total cost of the car. What is this amount?

   _____

2. The rate of interest on the car loan is 16% on the remaining cost of the car. What will this amount to for a one-year financing period?

   _____

3. The average number of miles driven per year is 15,000. What is the average miles driven per month?

   _____

4. Find the cost of fuel for your car choice by month. Use Fact Sheet II and deduct **5 miles** from the highest estimate when figuring your fuel mileage.

   $$\underline{\hspace{3cm}} \div \underline{\hspace{1cm}} \times \underline{\hspace{3cm}} = \underline{\hspace{3cm}}$$
   (miles per month)   (mpg)   (price of gas)   (cost of fuel per month)

5. What will be the average fuel cost per year for your model?

   _____

6. How much will car insurance and five oil changes cost you by the year?

   _____

7. What will car insurance and the cost of five oil changes amount to by the month?

_____

8. What is the total cost for your model by the month? by the year?

Car payments   _____

Insurance   _____

Oil changes   _____   _____
                                           (Total cost by month)
Fuel costs   _____
                                           _____
                                           (Total cost by year)

9. Is the year cost more than your budgeted amount for transportation?

_____

10. How much money have you saved from your transportation budget amount which can be deposited in your savings account?

_____

GROUP MEMBER SIGNATURES

_____   _____

_____   _____

_____

≈ **OBSERVATION SHEET** ≈

	Group Members			
Contributes ideas				
Asks for help				
Gives direction to group's work				
Encourages				
Checks to make sure everyone understands				
Praises				

Cooperative Typing?!*

LARRY GANNON

Mounds View,
MN

Cooperative learning in a senior high typing class? *Hey, you two, one of you use your left hand and the other use your right.* No, that's not the way it's done. But the key is to think in terms of binding a group together with common goals and a sense of positive interdependence while allowing for individual contribution and improvement.

I have applied these critical elements of cooperative learning to my high school typing classes in three ways:

1. **Timings.** At the beginning of the semester I have my typing students individually establish their base speed and accuracy rate. Later in their cooperative groups, they combine their scores; the group must improve its rate by 25% over the course of the quarter. This technique motivates everyone to contribute and allows a maximum of flexibility, especially if  someone is absent (which is a major problem in high school). I make sure the group charts constant and accurate data. Friendly competition may develop among groups but not between individuals.

2. **Formating:** After clarifying with the class the content being learned (i.e., a typical business letter), I require that the group acquires common knowledge on the topic. Once they are confident that all mem-

---

* Reprinted from **Our Link**, 1:5, April, 1983, p. 7

bers know the material, they set up their machines for the task using
an identical format, such as the same margin and tab settings. They
begin by each typing the first item in the letter. Then in round-
robin order, they each type the next letter part or paragraph, remove
the page, and pass it on to another group member. Four letters are
started simultaneously and the rotation is continued until four
similar letters are produced. Acceptable letters are those that have
appropriate margins and spacing formats. Of course, typo errors are
corrected. Upon completion of the four letters, credit is given to
each individual. The group's process is discussed and the students
attempt to define acceptable group behavior and effectiveness.

3. **Interdependence Based on Grades.** Within the quarter, I use three
    ways to create positive interdependence in my classes.
    - At first, the lowest grade earned within the group is assigned to
      every group member. This is harsh, but it does impress upon stu-
      dents the consequences of treating interdependence casually.
    - After a while, I prefer to average the scores and combine the
      group average with the individual score. This alters the
      individual's score but not greatly.
    - Sometimes I establish a bonus point system: If all group members
      score above a certain percentage, everyone earns bonus points.

  Cooperative learning has been very successful
     in typing class. My typing tip for the day:
        Always make sure the left hand
        knows what the right hand is doing!

Bonus Time

Cooperate to Lose Weight

ROY SMITH

Hingham,
MA

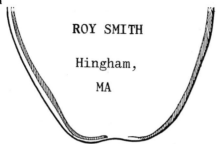

Dear Colleagues:

Did more than your stockings get stuffed this past vacation?

Can you pinch more than an inch?

In fact, can you crunch a bunch?

In short, are you creating a "heavy" scene?

Don't fret and don't despair -- for help is on the way! Join our revolutionary new six-week diet plan and win by losing. Here's how it works:

Object: Cooperate to lose weight

Time Period: Six weeks (i.e., Monday, January 7th, and ending Friday, February 15)

Procedures: 1. Sign up and weigh in at the nurse's office by Monday, the first day of the six weeks. Space is limited, so hurry!

2. You will be assigned randomly to a team consisting of four members.

3. As a group, you will attempt to reduce the group's weight by the final Friday. The group that sheds the most will be the winner.

4. Weekly Friday weigh-ins.

5. One-time entry fee of $5.00 payable by the end of the

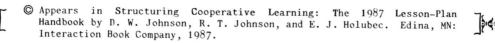

first week.

Remember: Your individual weight is your business. Only group totals
                 will be revealed as the contest progresses.

Rewa..:   1. Lost pounds
                 2. A free PIP for all teams on final Friday*
                 3. Winning team is reimbursed the entry fee
                 4. Winning team chooses the menu
                 5. Losing team prepares the feast

Bonus: A bottle of spirits or gourmet coffee blend for the high-
                 est individual weight loss from a contestant (excluding
                 members of the winning team)

* A surcharge will be imposed for team member's guests. PIP is a Pig-In
   Party at a place to be announced.

So come on and join the fun. What have you got to lose?
                         Something!
                 What have you got to gain?
                         Nothing!
         People won't think less of you for joining,
                 But they might SEE less!

Reprinted from: Structuring Cooperative Learning: Lesson Plans for
    Teachers by R. T. Johnson and D. W. Johnson.   Edina, MN: Interaction
    Book Company, 1984.

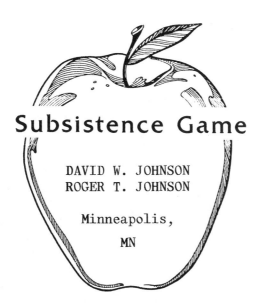

Subsistence Game

DAVID W. JOHNSON
ROGER T. JOHNSON

Minneapolis,
MN

This game simulates the effects of unequal resources in a group. It also allows for the development within the group of either cooperation or competition. It will be very important to process the group's interactions at the completion of the activity. The procedure is as follows.

1. Form groups of seven. One member should volunteer to be the recorder and another member should volunteer to be the observer. Each group should have five participants, one recorder, and one observer.

2. To play the game contained in this exercise the group needs a pack of blank food cards. The group also needs a pack of hunting and gathering cards (found at the end of the lesson).

3. The basic procedure of the game is as follows:

   a. Each participant receives three food cards.

   b. The recorder shuffles the hunting and gathering cards and places them in the center of the group.

   c. Each participant draws a card in turn (going counterclockwise), reads it to the group, and receives from or gives to the recorder the required number of food cards.

   d. The day's hunting and gathering is over when every participant has drawn one card. Participants may give any number of food cards to each other. At the end of the day they must give one food card to the recorder. Failure to do so results in death by starvation and dropping out of the game.

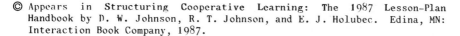

e. After seven rounds the week's hunting and gathering are over. Points are awarded to group members.

f. The game is played for a minimum of two weeks (14 rounds).

4. The role of the observer is to record the frequency of the behaviors listed on the observation sheet. The frequencies are reported to the group during the concluding group discussion.

5. The role of the recorder is to:

a. Read the Subsistence Instruction Sheet to the group.

b. Review the rules with participants.

c. Give each participant three food cards.

d. Shuffle the hunting and gathering cards and place them in the center of the group.

e. Distribute and collect food cards on the basis of the cards drawn.

f. At the end of each round collect one food card from each participant.

g. Ensure that each participant announces how many food cards s/he has at the end of each round.

h. Announce how many participants starved to death and who had the most food cards at the end of each week (seven rounds)

6. When the game is over, discuss the following questions:

a. Who survived and who died?

b. How was a cooperative or a competitive strategy decided on?

c. How did participants feel about the impending death by starvation?

d. How did the dead feel when they knew others could have saved them?

e. How did the survivors feel when others died when they had extra food cards?

f. Who organized the group to create a "just" distribution of food?

g. What real-life situations parallel this exercise?

SUBSISTENCE EXERCISE: Hunting and Gathering Cards

You found no food today.	Excellent shot! You killed a deer worth two days of food. You get two food cards from the recorder.
You made a beautiful shot at what looked like a deer, but it turned out to be a strangely shaped rock. You got no food today!	You met a member of another group and fell in love. To impress your new love, you gave him/her one day's food. Give recorder one food card. If you don't have a food card, and if no one will give you one, you die of starvation!
You shot a bird. You get one food card from the recorder.	You shot a snake. You get one food card from the recorder.
Wild dogs chased you and to get away you threw them one day's food. Give the recorder one food card. If you do not have a food card, and if no one will give you one, you die of starvation.	Army ants chased you and to get away you threw them one day's food. Give the recorder one food card. If you do not have a food card, and if no one will give you one, you die of starvation.
 You fell asleep and slept all day. You got no food today.	 You shot a lizard. You get one food card from the recorder.

SUBSISTENCE EXERCISE: Hunting and Gathering Cards

Excellent shot! You aimed at a bird you thought was standing on a rock. Your arrow hit the rock, which turned out to be a pig. You get two food cards from the recorder.	 You found some wild carrots. You get one food card from the recorder.
 You found a deer, but a bear scared it away before you could shoot at it. You got no food today.	You found an apple tree. Birds had eaten almost all of them. You get one food card from the recorder.
Excellent shot! Just as you shot at a deer, a wild pig ran in the way and got killed. You receive two food cards from recorder.	Excellent shot! You killed a wild pig. You get two food cards from the recorder. 
You shot a rabbit. You get one food card from the recorder.	While hunting, you accidently stepped on a snake and killed it. You receive one food card from the recorder.
 You found no food today. Probably too hot for anything to be out and around.	On the way home you fell into a swamp. You lost two day's worth of food to a hungry crocodile. Give two food cards to the recorder. If you do not have them, and if no one will give them to you, you die of starvation.

SUBSISTENCE EXERCISE: Hunting and Gathering Cards

While running away from a lion, you took refuge in a peach tree. You receive one food card from the recorder.	You found a nest of field mice and bopped them all on the head. You get one food card from the recorder.
You shot at a deer but missed. You got no food today! 	You found no food today.
 Lucky fluke! You shot at a deer and hit a rabbit. You get one food card from the recorder.	 You shot a bird. You get one food card from the recorder.
While you were hunting, a skunk broke into your hut and ate two days' worth of food. Give two food cards to the recorder. If you do not have two food cards, and if no one will give you one, you die of starvation.	You found a berry bush. Berries are in season. You get one food card from the recorder.
While you were hunting, a lion ate you and all your food. Give all your food cards to the recorder and drop out of the game. Since you didn't starve, group's points not affected. You are reborn the next week.	Lucky fluke! You shot at a wild pig and hit a rabbit. You get one food card from the recorder.

SUBSISTENCE EXERCISE: Hunting and Gathering Cards

Excellent shot! You killed a deer. You get two food cards from the recorder.

While hunting, you found a berry bush. Berries are in season. You get one food card from the recorder.

You found some wild lettuce. You get one food card from the recorder.

Best of luck! You found a deer with a broken leg. You killed it with your stone club. Two food cards!

You shot a rabbit. You get one food card from the recorder.

You looked and l o o k e d and l but found no food today!!

You shot a bird. You get one food card from the recorder.

You shot at a rabbit, but it but it zigged instead of zagged. You got no food today.

You shot an aardvark! You get one food card from the recorder.

You walked for M I L E S and found nothing to gather or shoot at. You got no food today.

INSTRUCTION SHEET

A severe drought has devastated your world. Because food is
so scarce, you have banded together into a hunting and
gathering group. It is more efficient for several people to
coordinate their hunting and gathering so that more
territory may be covered in any one day.
There are five members of your hunting
and gathering group. The food cards
in your hands represent all you have left of
your dwindling food supply. Since you already
are weakened by hunger, you must eat at the end
of each day (round) or die. At that time, you must
give up one food card. When you are out of cards, you
will die of starvation. A member who does not have one food
card at the end of a day (round) is considered to be dead and
can no longer participate in the group. Members with only one
food card may not talk. Only members with two or
more food cards may discuss their situation
and converse with each other. You may give
food cards to each other whenever you wish to
do so.

Johnson, Johnson and Holubec

$\mathcal{D}$ISCUSSION QUESTIONS

1. Who survived and who died?

2. How was a cooperative or a competitive strategy decided on?

3. How did participants feel about the impending death by starvation?

4. How did the dead feel when they knew others could have saved them?

5. How did the survivors feel when others died when they had extra food cards?

6. Who organized the group to create a "just" distribution of food?

7. What real life situations parallel this exercise?

RULES for SUBSISTENCE

1. The game begins when the recorder gives all participants three food cards, shuffles the hunting and gathering cards, and places them in the center of the group.

2. The purpose of the game is to gain points. You receive eight points if at the end of the week of hunting and gathering (seven rounds) you have more food cards than does any other participant in your group. If no one in your group has starved at the end of the week of hunting and gathering, all participants receive five points.

3. The game is played for a minimum of two weeks. At the beginning of each week all participants begin with three food cards and with all five participants alive.

4. You draw one card during each round. You read it aloud to the group and receive from or give to the recorder the number of food cards indicated.

5. During a round you may give food cards to other particpants if you wish to.

6. All participants read the hunting and gathering cards aloud. Only those with two or more food cards, however, may discuss the game with each other. Participants with one or no food cards must be silent.

7. At the end of each round participants hold up their food cards and announce to the group how many food cards they have.

8. At the end of each round participants give one food card each to the recorder. This symbolizes the food eaten during the day to stay alive.

9. If a participant cannot give a food card to the recorder at the end of a round, the participant dies of starvation and is excluded from further rounds during that week.

10. At the end of each week of hunting and gathering (seven rounds) the recorder announces who has the most food cards and how many participants starved to death. Points are then awarded.

RECORD SHEET

NAME	ROUND 1	ROUND 2	ROUND 3	ROUND 4	ROUND 5	ROUND 6	ROUND 7

OBSERVATION SHEET

	ROUND 1	ROUND 2	ROUND 3	ROUND 4	ROUND 5	ROUND 6	ROUND 7
NUMBER OF CARDS GIVEN AWAY							
NUMBER OF CARDS TAKEN AWAY							
NUMBER OF PEOPLE STARVED							
COOPERATIVE STRATEGY SUGGESTED							
COMPETITIVE COMMENT							
OTHER							

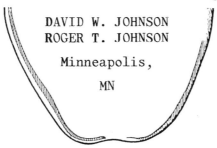

The High Achieving Student
in Cooperative Learning Groups

DAVID W. JOHNSON
ROGER T. JOHNSON
Minneapolis,
MN

To most educators, it is obvious that low- and middle-achieving students have much to gain by working in cooperative learning groups with high-achieving peers. In terms of motivation, actual achievement, and having positive peer models to emulate, the largest gainers from working in heterogeneous cooperative learning groups are the low-achievers and the next largest gainers are the middle-achievers.

What is not so obvious to many educators is that high-achieving students benefit in a number of ways from collaborating with low- and middle-achieving classmates. We and others around the country have conducted numerous studies comparing the achievement of high-, middle- and low-achieving students in cooperative, competitive, and individualistic learning situations (for specific references see Johnson & Johnson, 1983, 1985; Johnson, Maruyama, Johnson, Nelson, & Skon, 1981). Achievement consists of a number of dimensions, including daily performance, performance on final examinations, retention of the material learned over a period of weeks and months, level of reasoning strategies used, critical analysis, elaboration of the material being learned and networking it with previously learned material, and creativity of thought. A very conservative conclusion from the available research is that there is no evidence of high-achieving students being "pulled down" by participating in heterogeneous cooperative groups, and considerable evidence that high achievers are "pushed up."

The research results indicate that for performance on daily assignments and final and retention tests, high-achievers working in heterogeneous cooperative groups have never done worse than their counterparts working competitively and individualistically, and most often they do better. For aspects of achievement other than test scores, the benefits of learning within heterogeneous cooperative groups for high-achieving students are more apparent. High-achieving students more frequently use higher-level reasoning strategies, engage in deeper level and more critical analysis, derive more creative answers, and engage in more elaborative explanations when they learn in cooperative, as opposed to competitive or individualistic, learning situations. The cognitive processes involved in having to talk through and explain (perhaps in several different ways) the material being studied enhance retention and promote the development of higher-level reasoning strategies. It may be that bright students get quick, intuitive, correct answers to problems, but they may not have a conscious strategy for getting the answer. Material that is orally explained and tied into other conceptual frameworks is more effectively learned than material that is simply read.

There is growing evidence that a silent student is a student who is not engaging in all of the cognitive processes necessary for high-quality learning.

An equally important benefit for high-achievers participating in heterogeneous cooperative learning groups is the development of collaborative skills and friendships. While bright students are often resented and sometimes ostracized in a competitive setting, they are seen as desirable partners in a cooperative setting. The friendships formed in cooperative learning groups have important influences on such variables as self-esteem, psychological adjustment, and positive attitudes toward the subject area being studied. And in collaborating with middle- and low-achieving peers (as well as other bright students), high-achievers are more likely to develop the leadership, communication, decision-making, and conflict management skills needed for future career success.

Some suggestions for structuring high-achieving students more successfully into heterogeneous cooperative learning groups are as follows.

1. **Structuring role interdependence.** Some of the roles that promote high achievement are explaining how answers are derived, relating the material being learned to previously learned materials, and integrating the material into existing conceptual frameworks. The role of observer requires skills in tabulating and explaining data as well as giving groupmates feedback. These skills are often challenging to high achieving students.

2. **Adapting lesson requirements.** While assigning a high-achieving student to a heterogenous cooperative learning group, you will need to consider the appropriate criteria for success and be able to adapt the lesson to meet this criteria. Ways this can be done include:

a. Using different criteria for success for each group member.

b. Varying the amount each group member is expected to master.

c. Giving group members different lists, words, and problems and then using the average percentage correct as the group's score.

d. Using improvement scores.

3. **Ensuring constructive groupmates.** In order to promote the cognitive processes most conducive to high quality learning it may be helpful to carefully consider who should collaborate with high achieving students. While it is sometimes productive to have several high achieving students work together, usually it is more productive to match high achievers with middle- and low-achieving students who will push for explanations and elaboration of the material being learned. Highly creative students (who may not be high academic achievers) and highly interpersonally skilled students who are middle achievers may be good matches for high achieving students and encourage them to think divergently and relate to others skillfully.

4. **Rewarding interpersonal skills development.** High-achieving students may be accustomed to experiencing success on individual academic tasks with relatively little effort. The ability to collaborate effec-

tively with other students cannot be taken for granted. The evaluation of how effectively they interact within cooperative learning groups often provides new challenges to high-achieving students.

5. **Giving bonus points for enriching the learning of others.** Efforts made by high achieving students (as well as middle and low achievers) to enrich the learning of other members of their group may qualify for bonus points. This provides an incentive for high achievers to broaden their study of a topic in order to bring in material not included in the texts and course handouts.

6. **Creating clear positive interdependence.** Some high achievers will see little benefit in helping other students learn. They may be inappropriately competitive or lack the empathy necessary for collaborating with low achieving classmates. By ensuring that the positive interdependence is clear teachers can promote perceptions of mutuality and responsibility for others that will benefit high achievers considerably.

7. **Promoting academic acceleration to more advanced material.** There may be a few students who should be studying material far above their grade level. This may be accomplished by placing them in higher grades for certain subject areas during part of the day or by having them study advanced material in homogeneous cooperative groups.

REFERENCES

Johnson, D. W., & Johnson, R. T. (1983).   The socialization and achieve-
ment crisis: Are cooperative learning experiences the solution?   In
L. Bickman (Ed.), **Applied Social Psychology Annual 4.**   Beverly
Hills, CA: Sage Publications.

Johnson, D. W., & Johnson, R. T. (1985).   **Cooperative learning.**   New
Brighton, MN: Interaction Book Company.

Johnson, D. W., Maruyama, G., Johnson, R., Nelson, D., & Skon, L. (1981).
Effects of cooperative, competitive, and individualistic goal structures on achievement: A meta-analysis.   **Psychological Bulletin, 89,**
47-62.

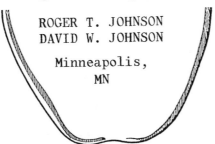

Monitoring Groups Effectively

ROGER T. JOHNSON
DAVID W. JOHNSON
Minneapolis,
MN

Monitoring students as they work cooperatively is the key to building more effective working relationships among students. In many ways, the teacher's job starts in earnest at this point, after teaching the material that needs to be taught directly -- when the small groups are "claiming" the ideas and concepts themselves (explaining, asking, arguing, relating, justifying their interpretations to one another). If the monitoring part of the cooperative model is boring to the teacher or is seen as a good time to grade papers or the teacher is feeling unnecessary, something is wrong with the way monitoring is set up.

There are three major tasks related to monitoring: providing task assistance, collecting data on students' behavior in the groups, and intervening to teach specific cooperative skills.

Task assistance is the most familiar of the monitoring activities. It includes clarifying instructions, finding other materials for groups to use, answering questions, etc. The interesting thing about task assistance is that much of what a teacher used to have to do when students were working alone is not gone. Students are asking each other those questions and should ask each other. Most teachers will not go to

a group unless everyone has his or her hand up -- as the first question will always be: Have you checked with your group? Make an effort to do less task assistance. Instead, turn your efforts to stirring up trouble in groups by asking questions, combining groups with different perspectives for a caucus, joining in with a minority opinion with support. The more cognitive dissonance you can get, the more thinking that is likely to result. Remotivation is part of your job and can be done with additional material handed out mid-stream, another tool to use, or the invention of another strategy to use. It may be that many groups are floundering around the same issue and you need to stop everyone to make a point or reteach a part of the lesson. However, the norm is the same with task assistance as it is with monitoring behaviors; don't intervene unless you have to.

Monitoring students' behavior in the groups is the primary job of the teacher when cooperation is new to students. You have specified a number of behaviors you want to see when students are working together cooperatively in your setting of the goal structure, and not need to see if those behaviors are actually there. Sometimes it is good to look for just one behavior that has been taught and encouraged. Sometimes it is good to monitor just one group or only a few groups as representatives of the class or because they need some special help. The more systematic the monitoring, the better the data, and the better the data, the more effective the feedback will be. We have developed a set of different observation sheets for classroom use and have a more elaborate set for our research studies. You may need to vary the procedure from day to day to make it challenging for yourself and keep you on your toes. Do whatever you have to do to get the data you need on the students' behaviors in the groups and to keep yourself active and up. We have tallied enough different behaviors that we now just code a group's behavior·in sequence. A sequence of I-P-Q-I-S-Ag means that Person 1 gave an idea, Person 2 para-

phrased the idea and Person 3 asked a question, Person 2 supplied an additional idea and Person 1 gave support; at that point the group agreed. This coding is very demanding and requires coding lots of different behaviors, but it challenges us and gives us very specific data to use in giving feedback and debriefing groups during the processing time. To add novelty to observing, use peer observers in each group or a roving peer observer (usually monitoring for one behavior, who talks or who gives support by using the phrases listed on the chart, etc.) A teacher in one of the classrooms we have worked with would inform the class that he had selected a "mystery person" to observe on that lesson as the class representative and that feedback on that student would be given at the end of class.

Intervening to teach cooperative skills is the best possible way to introduce new behaviors. If appropriate behavior can be supplied when it is needed in a specific way so that it can be immediately put into practice, the skill is seen as relevant and learned faster. However, intervening does not necessarily mean stopping a group on the spot and nailing members with the new skill. Another professor once said that he had three rules on intervening in groups:

1. When you feel like intervening, don't.

2. If you must, do it with a question, not an answer.

3. Move away as soon as you can (even if it's only three feet).

It is better to let students work things out for themselves than to become a walking, talking expert on human relations with students seeking you, or getting your help without seeking you, for every situation. American students are not getting enough changes in their daily lives at this point in history to solve their own interpersonal problems and invent the behaviors needed. Intervention can also be made at the beginning of the next class if there is a behavior that most of the groups could do more effectively, and perhaps assigned as a role in the group to insure its practice.

In a clearer way students need to be told that their behavior in the group is as important as the end product and these two things are highly related to one another. If the teacher is active when the students are working in their groups (monitoring with some care, turning questions back to the group, able to give specific, data-based feedback), this will give a message that the actual learning of the material and the interaction in the groups is important, perhaps even more important, than a test at the end.

SECTION VII

Resources

Recommended Materials

Books

Johnson, D. W. (1986). **Reaching Out: Interpersonal Effectiveness and Self-Actualization** (2nd ed.). Englewood Cliffs, NJ: Prentice-Hall.

Johnson, D. W. and Johnson, R. (1987). **Joining Together: Group Theory and Group Skills** (3rd ed.). Englewood Cliffs, NJ: Prentice-Hall.

Johnson, D. W. and Johnson, R. (1987). **Learning Together and Alone: Cooperative, Competitive, and Individualistic Learning** (2nd ed.). Englewood Cliffs, NJ: Prentice-Hall.

Johnson, D. W., Johnson, R., and Holubec, E. (1986). **Circles of Learning: Cooperation in the Classroom** (Revised Edition). Edina, MN: Interaction Book Company.

Johnson, D. W. and Johnson, R. T. (1987). **A meta-analysis of cooperative, competitive, and individualistic goal structures.** Hillsdale, NJ: Lawrence Erlbaum.

Teacher Materials

Johnson, D. W. and Johnson, R. T. (1985). **Cooperation in the Classroom.** Edina, MN: Interaction Book Company.

Johnson, D. W. and Johnson, R. T. (1985). **Cooperative Learning: Warm-Ups, Grouping Strategies and Group Activities.** Edina, MN: Interaction Book Company.

Movies

Johnson, D. W. and Johnson, R. T. (Producers), 1980. **Belonging.** 16mm film or VHS videotape, 27 minutes. Edina, MN: Interaction Book Company.

Johnson, D. W. and Johnson, R. T. (Producers), 1983. **Circles of Learning.** 16mm film or VHS videotape, 32 minutes. Edina, MN: Interaction Book Company.

Johnson, D. W. (1980). Group processes: Influences of student-student interactions on school outcomes. In J. McMillan (Ed.), **Social psychology of school learning.** New York: Academic Press.

Johnson, D. W. and Johnson, R. (1980). The key to effective inservice: Building teacher-teacher collaboration. **The Developer.** Oxford, Ohio: National Staff Development Council.

Johnson, D. W. and Johnson, R. (1985). Motivational processes in competitive, individualistic and cooperative learning situations. In C. Ames and R. Ames (Eds.), **Attitudes and Attitude Change in Special Education: Its Theory and Practice.** New York: Academic Press.

Johnson, D. W. and Johnson, R. (1984). Classroom learning structure and attitudes toward handicapped students in mainstream settings: A theoretical model and research evidence. In R. Jones (Ed.), **Special Education in Transition: Attitudes Toward the Handicapped** (118-142). ERIC Clearinghouse on Handicapped and Gifted Children: The Council for Exceptional Children.

Johnson, D. W., Johnson, R. and Maruyama, G. (1983). Interdependence and interpersonal attraction among heterogeneous and homogeneous individuals: A theoretical formulation and a meta-analysis of the research. **Review of Educational Research,** 52, 5-54.

Johnson, D. W., Maruyama, G., Johnson, R., Nelson, D., and Skon, L. (1981). Effects of cooperative, competitive, and individualistic goal structures on achievement: A meta-analysis. **Psychological Bulletin,** 89, 47-62.

Johnson, D. W. and Johnson, R. T. (1983). The socialization and achievement crisis: Are cooperative learning experiences the solution? In L. Bickman (Ed.), **Applied Social Psychology Annual 4.** Beverly Hills, CA: Sage Publications.

Johnson, D. W., Johnson, R. T. and Smith, K. A. (1985). Academic conflict among students: Controversy and learning. In R. Feldman (Ed.), **Social Psychological Applications to Education.** Cambridge University Press.

For further information call:
The Cooperative Learning Center
(612) 624-7031

Lesson Plan Guide

Subject Area:

Grade Level:

Lesson Summary: *This is a brief statement of the content of the lesson.*

Instructional Objectives: *List a few of the objectives you feel are most important in this lesson.*

Materials: *Please include a copy of all of the materials needed to complete the lesson. For example, if the lesson is a math lesson, include math problems and the answer sheet; if a reading comprehension lesson, include the copy of material to be read. If the material is copyrighted, send the reference and we will write for permission to reproduce the material.*

Time Required:

DECISIONS

Group Size: *Indicate an ideal group size for the lesson and a rationale for the number.*

Assignment to Groups: *Please indicate any special ways you have found effective in assigning students to groups and the reasons you have for a particular group composition such as needing a reader in each group or a mainstreamed student in each group or that random assignment helps the class get to know each other better.*

Roles: *List any roles which you find appropriate to the lesson. These may be either working roles (i.e., Reader, Recorder, Materials Handler) or skill roles (i.e., Encourager, Checker, Prober) or both.*

THE LESSON

Instructional Task: *The feedback we receive from teachers who are beginning to use cooperative groups is that the language you use to explain this section to your students is critical to the success of the lesson. Along with your commentary here, you may want to put in quotation marks the* statements you would make to the students.

Positive Interdependence: *How do you communicate to your students that they "sink or swim" together?*

Individual Accountability: *How do you make the students aware that each member of the group is responsible for learning the material?*

Criteria for Success:

Expected Behaviors: *This section of the lesson indicates how you convey to your students that they will be working cooperatively. Again, you may want to put in quotation marks the statements you would make to your students.*

MONITORING AND PROCESSING

Monitoring: *This step refers to the procedure you establish for yourself as a means of making systematic observations of students as they work in the groups. These observations are for you and are essentially a feedback system to you and to your students about what to look for when the students are working together, what the next skill to teach might be, or a way of judging how social skills have improved. You may want to write this in a general way or specify specific skills you watch for in your students' age group.*

Intervening: *Indicate any interventions you have made in the past when you did this lesson. If this is a lesson you saw someone else do, indicate the interventions made by the teacher or some interventions you thought would have been appropriate.*

Processing: *How do you give feedback on what you observed? Do you use a chart or give examples of effective behavior? How do you let your students know that you are observing them?*

How do you have your students process their interactions? What questions do you ask to get the group to process? Examples of different statements made for students in their age group are very useful to new cooperative teachers. You might also include sheets that students fill out or checklists that they use.

Ending: *How do you wrap up this lesson?*

AUTHOR'S NOTE

This is an optional addition in which you should feel free to insert any anecdotal comments on the lesson or tips which would make it even more effective.

We'll look forward to seeing your lessons!

Contributors

Carol Baldree

Watkins Junior High
Cypress-Fairbanks I.S.D.
P.O. Box 40040
Houston, TX 77240

Diane Browne

6624 Waterman Avenue
Hopkins, MN 55343

Mary Carnicelli

455 Oakridge Road
Auburn, NY 13021

Janet Clausi

c/o Greenwich Public Schools
Havemeyer Building
Greenwich Avenue
Greenwich, CT 06830

Jean Crockett

Emily Carr Elementary School
Vancouver, British Columbia
Canada

Tom Egan

Park Junior High
St. Louis Park Public Schools
6425 W. 33rd St.
St. Louis Park, MN 55426

Larry Gannon

Mounds View Senior High
Mounds View Public Schools
2959 Hamline Avenue N.
Roseville, MN 55113

Carol Goltz

West Anchorage High School
Anchorage School District
4600 DeBarr Avenue
Anchorage, Alaska 99502

Lucille Groulx

Loy Norrix High School
Kalamazoo, MI 49008

Ed Harris

Parkwood South School
St. Louis Public Schools
St. Louis, MO

Edythe Johnson Holubec

Box 552
Taylor, TX 76574

David W. Johnson

Cooperative Learning Center
202 Pattee Hall
150 Pillsbury Drive, SE
Minneapolis, MN 55455

Roger T. Johnson

Cooperative Learning Center
202 Pattee Hall
150 Pillsbury Drive, SE
Minneapolis, MN 55455

Nancy Killgore

Central Elementary School
Snohomish Public Schools
Snohomish, WA 98290

Glady Laughlin

2655 S. El Camino Road
Las Vegas, Nevada 89102

Tom Morton

4091 Dunbar
Vancouver, British Columbia
Canada V6S 2E5

Karen Schroeder

Lincoln Public Schools
720 S. 22nd
Lincoln, Nebraska 68510

Hildy Shank

Meadowbrook School
Hopkins Public Schools
5430 Glenwood Avenue
Golden Valley, MN 55422

Roy Smith

Central Junior High School
Hingham, MA 02043

Susan Snyder

Greenwich Public Schools
Havemeyer Building
Greenwich Avenue
Greenwich, CT 06830

Larry Stone

Tisbury School
Vineyard Haven, MA 02568

Lorry Szumylo

Meadowbrook School
5430 Glenwood Avenue
Golden Valley, MN 55422

Britt Vasquez

9560 Sierra College Boulevard
Roseville, CA 95678

Susan Ward

Cyprus-Fairbanks I.S.D.
P.O. Box 40040
Houston, TX 77240

Susan Whalen

Glenville Elementary School
Greenwich Public Schools
Havemeyer Building
Greenwich Avenue
Greenwich, CT 06830

Nancy Whitson

Snohomish Public Schools
Snohomish, WA 98290

 **WE THANK THEM
FOR THEIR COOPERATION**

Index by Subject Matter